FOR QUEEN AND COUNTRY

By the same author

The Garrick Year
The Ice Age
Jerusalem the Golden
The Millstone
The Needle's Eye
The Realms of Gold
A Summer Bird-Cage
The Waterfall

Arnold Bennett
Wordsworth

Lady Susan, The Watsons and Sanditon by
Jane Austen (Ed.)

FOR QUEEN AND COUNTRY

🔲🔲🔲🔲🔲🔲

BRITAIN IN THE VICTORIAN AGE

🔲🔲🔲🔲🔲🔲

Margaret Drabble

A Clarion Book

The Seabury Press · New York

The Seabury Press, 815 Second Avenue, New York,
New York 10017

First American Edition 1979

Library of Congress Cataloging in Publication Data

Drabble, Margaret, 1939–
  For Queen and country.

  'A Clarion book.'
  Bibliography: p.
  Includes index.
  SUMMARY: A look at British culture during the
age of Queen Victoria.
  1. England–Civilization–19th century.   2. Victoria,
Queen of Great Britain, 1819–1901. [1. England –
Civilization – 19th century.   2. Victoria, Queen of
Great Britain, 1819–1901]   I. Title.
DA533.D7 1978   942.081   78–9682
ISBN 0-8164-3222-8

Printed in Great Britain

🔲🔲🔲🔲🔲🔲

CONTENTS

🔲🔲🔲🔲🔲🔲

꧁꧁꧁꧁꧁꧁

ACKNOWLEDGMENTS

꧁꧁꧁꧁꧁꧁

Acknowledgments are due to the following for permission to reproduce the colour and black and white plates: Art Gallery of New South Wales, Sydney, 12; The British Library, 19, 41a, 41b; Central Press Photos, 14; Chappell & Company, from *Sixty Years of British Music Hall* by John M. Garrett, 51; City of Birmingham Museums and Art Gallery, 4; City of Manchester Art Galleries, 7; Colman Foods, 1a; Country Life, 16; Courtauld Institute, London, 7, 23a, 23b, 36a; H.M. The Queen, *1*, 5, 10, 18; Illustrated London News, 3, 29; Charles Jerdein, *6*; A. F. Kersting, 43; Leeds City Council, 32; Lofthouse of Fleetwood Ltd, 1b; Mary Evans Picture Library, 26, 28, 56; The Mansell Collection, *5*, 11, 25, 33, 35, 36b, 39, 40, 55; The Museum of London, 13; National Monuments Record, 15, 27; The National Portrait Gallery, London, 44, 54; The National Railway Museum, York, *3*, 30; A. & F. Pears, Ltd, 4; Pitman Publishing Ltd, from *Collecting Pot Lids* by Edward Fletcher, 2; Radio Times Hulton Picture Library, 50; The Royal Academy of Art, London, 52; Olive Smith, 38; The Tate Gallery, London, 2, *8*, 9, 45, 47; The Victoria and Albert Museum, London, 6, 8, 17, 21, 24, 37, 46, 48, 49, 53.

Thanks are also due to Horst Kolo for photographing plates 9, 20, 31, 34, 42 and to Batsford Books and Bea Howe, author of *Antiques in the Victorian Home*, for the cutting from the *Ladies' Newspaper* reproduced as plate 22.

᠋᠋᠋᠋᠋᠋

INTRODUCTION

᠋᠋᠋᠋᠋᠋

THE first and most obvious point to make about the Victorian age is that it was very long. Victoria came to the throne in 1837, when she was only eighteen, and she reigned for sixty-four years, until her death in 1901. She gave her name to a period of immense change, and lived through many crises, both personal and national, so it is difficult to point to any one achievement or characteristic of her reign and say '*That* is typically Victorian'. In a short book like this, it would be easy to give an impression – and a perfectly fair one – that Victorian England was wealthy, progressive, adventurous, and energetic. But it would also be as easy to paint a world of desperate poverty, ill health, bad housing and hard labour. Both pictures are true. Similarly, we could see the Victorians as a pious, religious, church-going, devout people, enthusiastic builders of churches and chapels, keen writers and readers of sermons – or we could see them as a nation tormented by religious doubt and debate, living in a time when simple faith in God, the Bible and Christianity was being destroyed by scientific and historical discoveries. We could see them as people with a passion for machinery and industry and the progress they were thought to bring – or as nostalgic escapists, looking back with regret to the lost crafts and graces of the past.

In fact, we cannot speak of the Victorians as though they were one people. Disraeli, politician and novelist, rightly said that they were two nations, the rich and the poor, but there were many subdivisions within those two nations. Victoria not only ruled for a long time, she also presided over an enormous population explosion. The figures are staggering. During her life, Britain changed from a land with a small population of fifteen million, most of whom lived and worked in the country, to a nation of thirty-two million, most of whom lived and worked in the rapidly growing cities we know today – Manchester, Liverpool, Birmingham, Newcastle. The population more than doubled.

So the sheer size of the problem, when we begin to speak of the Victorian age as a whole, is almost overwhelming. How can a historian or a critic generalize about such a vast mass, in such a stage of transition? About so many far-reaching changes, the end of which we cannot see even today? Any picture I can give will inevitably be incomplete and personal; the subject is too big to tackle in any other way.

And yet, for various reasons, I think we do all share some sense of what we mean by the word 'Victorian' – which, incidentally, was not used by the Victorians themselves until Victoria had been on the throne nearly fifteen years. In many ways, they are very close to us. There are people alive today who remember the Diamond Jubilee of 1897, and nearly all of us have in our homes objects that date from her reign – books, knives and forks, photographs, furniture. Many people in Britain live in Victorian houses, go to Victorian schools, use letter-boxes, railway stations, park benches and shops that would have been familiar sights a hundred years ago. We can buy marmalade and mango chutney, anchovy paste and golden syrup, soap and matches, mustard and cough sweets (see plate 1), with the same brand names and almost the same containers and labels that our great-great-grandparents used to buy, for this was the first age of mass advertising and mass production. Some of the cheap everyday objects that the Victorians used to throw on their rubbish dumps have now become collectors' items – coloured glass bottles, beautifully decorated pot lids from toothpaste and meat paste containers (see plate 2). We can guess at life in the Middle Ages through historical reconstructions, and through carefully preserved cathedrals, paintings and manuscripts, but the Victorians are all around us, reminding us of themselves by millions of mass-produced, ordinary little objects, as well as by their grander

1. Victorian advertisement and label.

2. Victorian pot lids.

designs. Triumphs of engineering and civic pride, such as Paddington station and the Houses of Parliament in London, the Clifton suspension bridge at Bristol, are still with us, and so is Pears soap.

It would be hard to over-emphasize the importance of advertising as a means of transmitting images from generation to generation (see plate 3). Advertisements are important documents for the social historian, and they are also, as is now recognized, a genuinely popular art form, with a power greater than that of merely selling the product they display. Some images seem to catch the essence of an entire epoch. Take, for example, the famous painting of *Bubbles* by Millais (see plate 4), which was not originally intended as a poster at all; it was a painting of his grandson, and was exhibited at the Royal Academy, then sold to the *Illustrated London News*. Pears bought it and used it to advertise their soap, making it one of the most famous paintings in Britain; it is still used by them in overseas publicity. Recently, it has re-appeared as a design on plastic aprons and plastic bags. Clearly, it is an image that will never die. Surrounded by such memorials, we do not find it too difficult to picture at least some aspects of Victorian England – and perhaps one should also point out it is the first period of which we have photographic

3. A picture of Queen Victoria painted to advertise a popular product, a practice no longer allowed.

records. We have to rely on paintings and engravings for our impressions of earlier epochs, and although the camera can be selective too, it is less so than the individual artist.

4. Millais's *Bubbles*.

So we have a good picture of the way the Victorians lived. We have also inherited many of their attitudes. Our ideas of education and democracy, of religious tolerance, of work and money, of medicine, of family life, were all forged during this period. During Victoria's reign, all men (though not all women) won the right to vote, and all children the right to at least some education; religious minorities won civil rights. It is hard to imagine a time when the vast majority of Britons had no say whatsoever in how they were governed, when Catholics and women were debarred from university education, when children started work at the age at which they now start school. We benefit today from the legacy of the great reformers – men like Shaftsbury, Robert Owen, John Stuart Mill, Bradlaugh the atheist, Chadwick the sewage fanatic; women like Florence Nightingale and Emily Davies. They made the world we live in.

I think there is another reason why we have a clearer picture of what we mean by Victorian than of what we mean by Georgian or Jacobean, or even, to take a closer example, Edwardian. It is simple, but significant. *We all know who Victoria was.* Most of us tend to get mixed up when we think of the many kings called Henry, George and Edward, and have only the vaguest impression of Queen Anne, although there was only one of her: but we all know Victoria. (If her mother had continued to call her Alexandrina, which was her first Christian name, we would now be reading of the Alexandrine Age, which is unthinkable.) She lived long enough, and had a sufficiently forceful personality, to impose herself very thoroughly on the British imagination, and to impose her husband too – for who thinks of Victoria without Albert? The wives and consorts of other monarchs have vanished into oblivion, but Albert lives on, in the Albert Memorial, the Albert Bridge, the Albert Hall. She was determined we should not forget him. Together, they presented an extraordinarily powerful popular image, which changed the life style of a whole nation. So let us begin our examination of the age by an account of the effect that the Queen's personality had upon her subjects.

༒༒༒༒༒༒

VICTORIA AS QUEEN

༒༒༒༒༒༒

WIFE AND MOTHER

QUEEN VICTORIA was born in 1819, the only child of the Duke and Duchess of Kent. She was involved in politics from before her birth, for the Duke had married his Duchess, the daughter of the Duke of Saxe-Coburg, in a rather undignified rush to provide heirs to the throne, after the death of Princess Charlotte in 1817. Charlotte, only child of Prinny, the Prince Regent, had been the only heir. So the Duke, who was one of the seven sons of George the Third (none of whom had any legitimate children) left the woman with whom he had been quietly and happily living for many years, and got married as the state required. The Duchess duly produced Victoria; the Duke, his duty finished, died a few months later. So Victoria's childhood was overshadowed by the possibility that she might succeed to the throne; it was not a certainty, for some of her uncles might yet produce children. But her mother, and her German governess Lehzen, kept the prospect in their minds, and gradually it became clear to others, if not to herself, that she would eventually become Queen. She had a lonely childhood, carefully protected, surrounded by threats of intrigue; maybe she was aware that she was being manipulated for the advantage of others in a political game taking place far above her head. If so, she lived to have her revenge. She was used as a puppet, but even as a small child she resisted the role, and was famed for her stubborn temper. Her life could hardly have been natural; friends and companions had to be carefully selected, and not by her. She played with dolls, like many little girls, but did not like baby dolls that she could mother – she preferred dolls dressed as adults. Maybe, in cataloguing and organizing and arranging them, she felt she was retaliating against the adult world that was using her.

She was eleven when she was told she was to succeed to the throne. George the Fourth was on the point of death; his successor, her uncle William (William IV) was already sixty-five, and it seemed unlikely that he would now produce any children. Victoria's reaction to the news is celebrated; 'I will be good,' she said, according to her governess.

And she was good. She worked hard, kept a diary in which she was tactfully very civil about everyone who might read it, was polite and docile. After seven years William died, on 20 June 1837, and she found herself Queen. She survived the shock with dignity, and observers commented on the 'self-possession' with which she confronted her coronation, and later the affairs of state. But she was very young indeed. Older statesmen and members of the Court described her in affectionate but slightly patronizing terms; Lord Holland called her 'a very nice girl', and Lady Granville said she was 'such a little love of a Queen!' How was a nice eighteen-year-old girl going to manage as head of state?

Luckily, she at once found a useful ally in her Prime Minister, Lord Melbourne, who adapted himself quickly to the new Court, spending many evenings with her playing nursery games such as spillikins and draughts and 'dissected pictures' (dissected pictures were an early form of jigsaw). She adored Melbourne, finding in his polite attention and kindness the father she had never known. Some historians have mocked at the schoolroom atmosphere which she created around her, and which lasted well into her married life; she and Albert enjoyed family games and practical jokes rather than clever conversation. But when she came to the throne she was, after all, a schoolgirl, and one who had seen even less of life than most. It was natural for her to react against the insecurity of her infancy and the intrigue and ambition that had hung around her from birth. She wanted safety, to be surrounded by friends; she wanted loyalty and pleasantness and familiar faces. And she was obstinate in her desires: she was to rock the government in 1839 and oust the new Prime Minister, Sir Robert Peel – who was a Tory – by insisting on keeping all the trusted ladies of her Household, who were Whigs, and some of whom would traditionally have been replaced under a change of political power. Such persistence made her deeply unpopular in some quarters, but she seems to have had a confidence that made her indifferent to most criticism, and was never afraid of asserting her own standards. She hated, and continued all her life to hate, scandal, fast living, swearing, gambling, drinking and smoking; her consistency compelled respect even from the reluctant.

In part, again, her emphasis on high moral standards was a reaction against the age that had gone before. She had been brought up in a world where it was considered normal for dukes and kings to keep mistresses. During the Regency, manners were coarse, aristocratic language was peppered with oaths, and it was customary for gentlemen to drink so much each evening that they ended up under the table, and to eat so much that they became grotesquely fat; according to one observer, Prinny's belly, when he undid his stays, reached his knees. Victoria turned with disgust from this age of debauchery, and one can hardly blame her for it; on the other hand, one cannot help feeling sympathy as well as admiration for Lord Melbourne, an intelligent, sophisticated man, forced to spend his evenings playing spillikins. But maybe he too could see the advantages of a safe, quiet fireside – he himself was illegitimate, his marriage to the notorious Lady Caroline Lamb had been a disaster, he had featured in two divorce actions, and his only son was mentally retarded. Perhaps he found the new régime at Buckingham Palace restful after the passions of private life and politics; he was fifty-eight, getting old, touched by the adoration and dependence of his new young sovereign.

Decorous though she was, Victoria was capable of enjoying herself. She loved riding and dancing, and in 1839 she demonstrated that she had strong emotions by falling in love with her German cousin, Albert. On the whole, kings and queens do not expect to marry for love. Victoria was certainly conscious of her own position, and of the need to make useful alliances, but not even her most hostile critics have suggested that she did not love Albert. At the end of his first visit in 1836 she wrote in her Journal with great enthusiasm, 'It was the last time we were at the Opera with my dear Uncle and my *dearest, most beloved* cousins . . . dearest Ernest and dearest Albert are very clever, naturally clever, particularly Albert . . .' This may or may not have been love at first sight; certainly, when he returned on a second visit in 1839, she was so struck by him that she proposed to him within a week. He accepted. She was enraptured. 'Oh, when I look in those lovely, lovely blue eyes, I feel they are those of an angel,' she wrote.

And so began one of the most famous of royal marriages. It was immensely popular, particularly with the new middle classes, who loved Victoria and Albert; some of the older aristocracy were more hesitant, uncertain whether Albert would learn to be a proper hunting, shooting English gentleman; but for the majority the couple stood for the solid virtues of home and fireside, with an added dash of romance. They were young, good-looking, and in love, and to marry for love, dignified by the romantic novels and poems of the time, was the ideal, if not always the practice, of ordinary people. The new Queen made a good heroine and a good model. Previous sovereigns had lived in a world apart, and not a very attractive one at that, but Victoria and Albert lived simply, kept early hours, worked hard, loved dogs and horses and little children, enjoyed skating and tobogganing and country picnics and dances, just like their hard-working subjects. Yet at the same time they were sufficiently glamorous, fabulously wealthy, able to command every luxury of an ever-expanding and prosperous empire. They were a symbol, much as the Queen is now, of both the ordinary and the exotic. Their subjects were able to identify with them, while preserving a feeling of awe and devotion. It had been a long time since the country had had such a suitable figurehead.

Royal family portraits catch exactly this mixture of grandeur and happy, domestic, informal cosiness. Landseer's portrait of

Windsor Castle in Modern Times (see colour plate 1) shows the handsome Albert in dashing boots, very much the sportsman, with an array of dead birds he has shot; he is watched with an appearance of humble admiration by his Queen, while the little Princess Royal, their eldest child, plays, rather unsuitably to a modern eye, with the corpse of one of his little victims. Dogs, beloved by the royal family then as now (and favourite subjects of Landseer, who preferred painting animals to people) join in their tribute to the Prince, adding a touch of comedy. Victoria found this picture 'very cheerful and pleasing', and despite the corpses, it does show a happy family intimacy. But we cannot forget for a moment that we are in the presence of royalty; the clothes and furnishings are rich and sumptuous, and beyond the window stretch the extensive formal gardens of the Castle. A slightly later painting, by the court painter Winterhalter, dates from 1846, and shows the couple with five of their children (see plate 5); from left to right, we see little Alfred, wearing the skirts that boys wore until they were six or seven, and Edward, the Prince of Wales, leaning on his mother's knee, showing no sign in his innocent boy's face of the trouble he was to become; Princess Alice leans over baby Helena from one side, and Vicky, the eldest, gazes protectively down from the other – again, a happy family group, although we note that the royal couple are here older, in Victoria's case noticeably plumper, and that both are wearing formal dress and decorations, and sitting as upright as the scene permits upon their regal chairs. The family was much painted, and one could choose illustrations from a wealth of material, but perhaps, as a contrast, we should include Roger Fenton's photograph, taken in 1854 (see plate 6). There is little grandeur here at all, but a great deal of humanity; the Queen is looking tense and a little anxious, perhaps perturbed by the relatively new ordeal of photography, and this time it is Albert's turn to look at her with admiration and reassurance. Both of them look remarkably ordinary, like any prosperous middle-class couple of the day; the background is plain, Albert's clothes distinctly so. He holds a roll of papers in his hand, as though about to depart for the office and a day's work. There is something

5. Winterhalter's painting of Victoria and Albert and their young family.

touching about the sprigged pattern of the Queen's dress; she looks here vulnerable, dependent, without her badges of office. We seem to glimpse them as they really were, for a moment. They look as though they are alone together, cut off from the rest of the world. And so, no doubt, they felt at times; theirs was a remarkably close marriage, and they confided in one another and looked to one another for advice, loyalty and comfort.

The institution of marriage took on a new dignity from the royal example, and the home took on a new dignity too, as the sacred shrine that housed it. The Dickensian Christmas-card-picture of fun by the fireside, of party games round the Christmas tree, dates from Victoria's reign, as indeed do Christmas cards and Christmas trees themselves, both of which were imports from the continent. Christmas trees, which we now consider traditional

6. Roger Fenton's photograph of Victoria and Albert.

here, had long been popular in Germany, and Albert's royal blessing helped to establish them as part of our way of life. The idea of cosiness and buttered toast by the fireside, of shutting out the hard world outside, is hardly an image of majesty, but it is one that Victoria and Albert patronized. Novels and paintings of the period love to paint a picture of homely comfort or gaiety: *Mr Fezziwig's Ball* (see plate 7) expresses the rather childish spirit of fun in which Dickens revelled, and by all accounts

Albert and Victoria were as happy playing Blind Man's Buff with
the children as they were at the grandest opera.

One of the reasons why the Victorians were so fond of the
home was that the outside world was so cold, dirty and dis-
agreeable; no wonder they took refuge, if they were lucky enough
to be able to do so, in a warm padded sanctuary. The Victorian
home was, literally, padded in a way that the homes of previous
ages had not been; the coiled spring that makes our beds and

7. *Mr Fezziwig's Ball*, from Dickens's *A Christmas Carol*, drawn by John Leech.

chairs so comfortable was not invented until 1828. Chairs before that were hard to sit on; the large armchairs and settees in which gentlemen lounged at home or in their second home, the club, were a relatively new innovation. (Ladies were still not supposed to lounge, and indeed their clothes would have made any such indulgence difficult, but paintings often show the man of the house sprawling at ease.) A beautiful illustration of padding can be seen in the royal railway carriage, which was built in 1869 (see colour plate 3); it is as well-upholstered, cushioned, fringed, buttoned and embroidered as a mobile Victorian drawing-room, a perfect refuge from the miraculous but alarming invention of the railway.

The respectability which overtook polite society in the second half of the nineteenth century was not of course created single-handed by the Queen. Others before her had tried to 'clean up' the licentiousness they saw around them. We can see the shift towards politeness in the work of Jane Austen, who died in 1817, two years before Victoria's birth. As a child and young girl she was outspoken and carefree, but the vicar's daughter who enjoyed rolling down grassy banks and playing charades in the barn grew up to write *Mansfield Park*, whose heroine thinks amateur theatricals are 'improper'. The efforts of Thomas Bowdler were another sign of changing times; he made himself immortally ridiculous in 1818 by producing a family Shakespeare which left out all the rude passages, thus leaving his name to the language in the verb 'to bowdlerize'. One must remember that the Victorians, including Victoria and Albert themselves, were fond of reading aloud to one another in the evenings, which meant that novels and poems had to be suitable for the whole family, young ladies and children included. The idea of what was suitable became increasingly strict; Fielding's novels, which had been widely admired fifty years earlier, were condemned as coarse and indelicate, as were Shakespeare's comedies. Charlotte Brontë, another well-bred vicar's daughter, was startled to find her own novels considered unsuitable reading matter for young girls.

In art galleries, ladies were advised to avert their eyes from classical nudes, although classical ones were naturally considered much more proper than modern ones, and a tradition of sculpting and painting naked models in the guise of Greek gods and goddesses persisted, even through the dark ages of prudery. But prudery at times went to exaggerated lengths; Edmund Gosse, in his autobiography *Father and Son*, tells the story of Susan Flood, a shoemaker's daughter, who was converted to the faith of the Plymouth Brethren. She was taken to the sculpture gallery at the Crystal Palace (an exhibition which had met with royal approval), where 'her sense of decency had been so grievously affronted, that she had smashed the naked figures with the handle of her parasol, before her horrified companions could stop her'. The Brethren agreed that her conduct had been magnificent. This Philistinism towards art persisted after Victoria's reign; in E. M. Forster's *A Room with a View* (1908) we find the heroine's chaperone, Miss Bartlett, persuading Lucy not to buy a photograph of Botticelli's *Birth of Venus* because 'Venus, being a pity, spoilt the picture, otherwise so charming'. (A 'pity' in art of course signified the nude.)

Philistinism, incidentally, is a word popularized in English by Matthew Arnold; the Philistines, to him, were the wealthy middle classes, who cared nothing for art and culture, placed too high a value on rigid moral standards, and believed that 'our greatness and welfare are proved by our being very rich'.

Some manifestations of the spirit of decency were less comic and more sinister than Susan Flood's; what can we make of the common objection to providing education for the poor, on the grounds that if the poor learned to write, they might shock the more genteel by scribbling rude words on walls?

Fear of the human body, accompanied by extreme modesty of dress, reached ridiculous proportions in the nineteenth century, though again the trend had been set before Victoria's reign: trousers were already known as 'unmentionables' in 1830, and the phrase 'nether person' was in use in 1835 to describe some offensive region of the body. (Both are excellent examples of the figure of speech known as a euphemism.) As the century wore on, modesty became more and more easily offended. The female leg seemed to cause a particular degree of alarm, and of course, the more thoroughly legs were covered, the more shocking they became. (As though in some kind of counter-balance, the bosom was much exposed, at least in the evening dress of fashionable society.) It is widely believed that Victorian housewives covered their tables and pianos with fringes and cloths because they found even furniture legs objectionable, but I haven't been able to find any contemporary confirmation of this; it seems to me more likely that the habit of draping every possible object in a room was another illustration of the Victorian love of clutter and bric-à-brac.

Extreme prudery could not help but have its effect on the female mind. It prevented (as it still prevents) many women from seeking adequate medical care, and it made childbirth even more dangerous than it already was, in those unhygienic days before the discovery of antiseptics. Although the Queen was constantly portrayed as a symbol of successful motherhood, she dreaded having babies, which is possibly why she did not much like them when they were very small; when her eldest daughter married and wrote to tell her mother she was pregnant, Victoria wrote back not, as one might have expected, with congratulations, but complaining of 'the horrid news'.

> What you say of the pride of giving life to an immortal soul is very fine, dear, but I own I cannot enter into that; I think much more of our being like a cow or a dog at such moments . . . (15 June 1858)

The extremely unnatural clothes that women wore in those days, together with the ignorance in which most girls were kept about the facts of life, made marriage and motherhood unnecessarily frightening. Ladies were not supposed to enjoy a happy sexual life, and no doubt, in the circumstances, many of them did not. Girls were taught to think of themselves as frail and delicate creatures. When the movement for higher education for women began, it was seriously argued by its opponents that women were physically unfit for too much study. Most attempts to liberate women from their confined existence met with the same difficulties; although the Queen dreaded having babies (and she had nine in all, a fair average for the time) she thought any mention of birth control even more 'horrid'. Efforts to spread information about this important subject aroused violent opposition; in 1860 the free thinker, Bradlaugh, and Mrs Annie Besant were tried and imprisoned for publishing a book on it. (The book sold 500 copies in its first twenty minutes on sale, which shows how badly it was needed.)

It is hard to defend the Victorians from the charge of hypocrisy so often levelled against them in this area. They allowed themselves to be shocked by the wrong things. One of the most popular mass-produced little figures of the day, which sat on many an over-loaded mantelpiece, was John Bell's *Dorothea* (see plate 8); she

8. John Bell's *Dorothea*.

also appears as an ornamental gas bracket. As she is dressed as a shepherd in historical costume, she is allowed to show more leg than most Victorian girls dared to display, except in their fairly discreet bathing dresses. (She is in fact a character from *Don Quixote*.) Her popularity undoubtedly springs from her attitude of discreet provocation. Yet the same people who complacently admired this figure in their drawing-rooms allowed themselves to be horrified by a real glimpse of leg on a real working girl. Reading the reports of inspectors investigating working conditions, we are today appalled by the hardship that women and children suffered; so, it is true, were the inspectors themselves, but they still reacted in a curious way to matters that seem to us, in comparison with the real problems, extremely trivial. One writes, of a group of turnip pickers in 1867, 'when the crops are wet, they tuck up their dresses between the legs, often leaving the legs much exposed'; another, of women in the brick-fields, 'Clad in a few dirty rags, their bare legs exposed far above the knees, their hair and faces covered with mud, they learn to treat with contempt all feelings of modesty and decency . . .' A third writes indignantly, 'I have seen boys bathing in the brooks, and girls between 13 and 19 looking on from the bank' – to which one can only say, thank goodness these little child labourers had some time off for a swim, or to stand and stare. Here we see two nations indeed; one of women so frail that a few hours of study in a university would be too exhausting, another of female labourers who worked from eight in the morning to five in the evening every day, sometimes longer, for eightpence a day, and who had to walk several miles to and from work each morning and evening.

Perhaps the most serious criticism one can make of Victoria as Queen is that she seems to have been indifferent to, though possibly not unaware of, the plight of so many of her subjects. Her indifference allowed her more prosperous citizens to maintain theirs. She endorsed the spirit of complacent hypocrisy, which tended to shut its eyes when confronted by anything indelicate or unpleasant. Her lack of initiative and real understanding made the task of the reformers much more difficult.

WIDOWHOOD: THE YEARS OF MOURNING

Victoria spent the first twenty-four years of her reign as a model wife; she was to spend the last forty as a model widow. One of the wealthiest and most powerful women in the world, she had played the part of devoted wife as well as any of those loyal women we see in Victorian paintings, whose main task seems to be to support and cherish their husbands. The work by George Elgar Hicks called *Woman's Mission: Companion to Manhood*, with its submissive wife supporting her husband in his loss (he is holding a black-edged announcement of bereavement, an object much loved by artists of the day), illustrates clearly the part that wives were supposed to play (see plate 9). And despite the paradox of her superior status, Victoria had fulfilled her mission with sincerity. She depended more and more on Albert, and submitted willingly to his judgement. He wrote her letters and dispatches for her, and she never chose a dress or a bonnet without asking his advice. No wonder she had little patience with the women who were campaigning for the right to vote and the right to work. She was a living embodiment of a happy wife who cannot imagine the problems of those who have no husband, want no husband, or need to escape from the unsuitable husband that they have. To her, Albert was perfection, and her marriage a triumphant success, without which she would never have been able to shoulder the burden of the Empire. And then, in 1861, after some months of exhaustion and illness, he died, killed by what was probably typhoid fever from the long-condemned drains of Windsor Castle. She was only forty-two. His death threw her into 'a dreadful agony', and those close to her wondered how she would survive the loss.

Her response was to fling herself into the deepest and most prolonged mourning, and to preserve the memory of Albert as though he were a saint or a martyr. The picture of her as a widow in black is as familiar to us as the pictures of her and Albert in their days of glory. She dedicated herself to perpetuating his memory by publishing his speeches, by arranging for a biography, by approving countless pictures, statues and busts, by placing a

9. George Elgar Hicks's *Woman's Mission: Companion to Manhood.*

memorial tablet at the spot where he shot his last stag and, most
conspicuously, by commissioning the Albert Memorial (see plate
43), that extraordinary monument which still stands, a familiar
landmark, in London's Kensington Gardens. Lytton Strachey, in
his 'debunking' book on her, claims that the suite of rooms Albert

had occupied at Windsor was kept exactly as it had been during his life, and that she commanded that 'her husband's clothing should be lain afresh, each evening, upon the bed, and that, each evening, the water should be set ready in the basin as if he were still alive; and this incredible rite was performed with scrupulous regularity for nearly forty years'. True or not, this is the kind of myth encouraged by the behaviour of the widowed Queen.

Her response would not have seemed as peculiar to her people as it does to us, for the Victorian attitude to death was very different from ours – though even then, her subjects began to grow impatient with her endless grieving, and *Punch* cartoons begged her to return to normal life. A period of deep mourning was, however, fashionable and obligatory. It had its own rigid rules. One would wear different clothes for the loss of a cousin, a second cousin, an aunt, an aunt by marriage. Posed photographs of sorrowing relatives around the gravestone or a bust of the departed are common; there are many of Victoria and the royal household (see plate 10). There was a prosperous trade in funeral fashions and mourning jewellery; jet from Whitby was particularly popular. Memorial cards with black edges, decorated with patterns of ivy, angels, weeping willows and broken columns, were as popular as Valentines and Christmas cards. Hair jewellery, made from hair of the loved one (see plate 11), had gone out of fashion by the death of Albert, but was still much worn in the early part of Victoria's reign. Victoria herself had a whole selection of mourning handkerchiefs, white (which was considered deeper mourning than mauve or grey) embroidered with black borders and monograms – and one quaintly embroidered with black and white tear drops.

Extreme mourning was not her personal invention, but her behaviour set a seal of approval on it, and was partly responsible for the death industry criticized in *The Times* (2 February 1875). It complains of 'prodigious funerals, awful hearses drawn by preternatural quadrupeds, clouds of black plumes, solid and magnificent oak coffins . . .' Such expensive pomp used to be reserved for the great; the Duke of Wellington's funeral, in 1852, had been a fantastic display, and drew enormous crowds. Now,

10. A formally composed group: Victoria's family photographed in front of a bust of their dead father.

11. Victorian mourning brooch, decorated with the hair of the dead relative.

however, says *The Times*, the fashion is spreading down through society. The new middle classes expect to be buried and mourned in the same style as their betters. The undertakers, naturally, did not complain.

Such interest in death, morbid to us, is not surprising. Life was more uncertain then than it is now. Mothers expected to lose some of their babies, many women died in childbirth, and the life expectancy of a working man was shockingly low. Widows accounted for a much higher percentage of the population than they do now; one estimate has it that in 1851, twelve women out of every hundred over the age of twenty were widows, and the proportion was still much the same at the 1901 census. (The widowers, presumably, remarried.) So there were plenty of Victoria's subjects who could identify themselves with her loss. The great killer was disease. The cholera epidemics of 1832, 1846–9, 1853 and 1865 killed many thousands. Typhoid, tuberculosis, small-pox and scarlet fever, now rare, were an ever-present threat. Understanding of hygiene was so poor that these illnesses attacked the rich as well as the poor, though more of the poor succumbed because of bad nutrition and bad housing. But the drains of Windsor proved as fatal as the slums of Gray's Inn Road. It was not until 1883 that the cause of cholera was identified, and doctors were often as much of a danger as a help to their patients, spreading disease by unwashed hands and dirty instruments. Lying-in hospitals, where the poor produced their babies, were particular sources of infection; it was safer to have babies at home.

So the Victorians comforted themselves, as best they could in the midst of this uncertainty, by elaborate rituals of grief. The popularity of the subject of death in art is to us astonishing. H. A. Bowler's *The Doubt: Can these dry bones live?* is typical, and shows a young and beautiful widow, leaning, melancholy, on a gravestone, staring at bones and a skull, and pondering no doubt on the possibility of reunion beyond the grave (see colour plate 2). The painting incidentally and unintentionally illustrates the insanitary and overcrowded condition of graveyards, already acknowledged by more advanced medical opinion as a cause of the high death rate. More shocking is Luke Fildes' *The Widower*, also much reproduced, which portrays genuine anguish (see plate 12). The deaths of children were often depicted in literature and art; everyone has heard of the death of Little Nell, and artists like Fildes and Frank Holl painted many dying infants and bereaved parents. In the Tate Gallery we can see Fildes' *The Doctor*, which shows a doctor bending over a sick child, the mother in despair in the background: Holl's *Hush* and *Hushed* show similar harrowing domestic death-bed scenes. Holl also painted *The First Born*, an idyllic portrayal of a village funeral. Many of these works seem to us excessively sentimental in treatment; a few hint at the real pain of loss, and a real questioning of providence.

Mournful sentimentality is one way of dealing with grief: another way is laughter. The literature of the period is full of jokes and cartoons about women who care more for looking elegant in black than for their lost ones, and it is hard to take some of the advertisements for mourning very seriously: in *The Queen* (7 May 1881) there is a picture of a young lady trying on a pair of black gloves at 1*s*. 11*d*. a pair, and the caption reads 'How small these gloves make my hands look!' Dickens, who can be as sentimental as any Victorian on the theme, can also be very off-hand about it: he describes a visit with his nurse when he was a little boy, to a lady

> who had had four children (I am afraid to write five, though I fully believe it was five) at a birth. This meritorious woman held quite a reception in her room on the morning when I was introduced there, and . . . the four (five) deceased young people lay, side by side, on a clean cloth on a chest of drawers; reminding me by a homely association, which I suspect their complexion to have assisted, of pigs' feet as they are usually displayed at a neat tripe shop.

A subscription is got up for the poor mother, but the young Dickens, with his keen nose for hypocrisy, refused to part with his pocket-money. The Victorians, prudish though they were, enjoyed the macabre, and stories of murders, violent death, and executions were widely read.

12. *The Widower* by Samuel Luke Fildes.

Victoria herself was never one to use humour as a defence, but even her sorrow did not last forever. She emerged and took her place in the public eye again, laying the foundation stone for Florence Nightingale's new hospital, St Thomas's, in 1868, attending the opening of the Albert Hall in 1871, accepting the title of Empress of India in 1877, and finally restoring court life to normal when she attended her son Arthur's wedding in 1879, wearing the Koh-i-Noor diamond and a dress with a train. But she still needed somebody to lean on. The Prince of Wales, who should have been the person to play this part, was rejected; she distrusted his character, and kept power from him for as long as possible. She blamed him in part for Albert's death; he and the Prince had quarrelled bitterly in 1860 over some indiscreet adventure of Edward's. She found it hard to forgive him for adding this extra anxiety to Albert's overworked last years, and disliked, with good reason, the 'fast set' of Marlborough House who were his friends. They stood for everything she and Albert had tried to remove from court life – scandal, drinking, high living, heavy gambling, debts.

The first companion she favoured was a curious choice. He was her Highland servant, John Brown, who was invited down from Balmoral in 1864 to encourage the Queen to start riding again. He became, to the irritation of the royal children, a close friend, and his intimacy with the Queen caused a certain amount of the scandal of which she herself so much disapproved. He was allowed to address her more informally than any other servant, and even shared the royal box at the opera. She later found another more suitable ally in her Tory Prime Minister, Disraeli, who became to her in her widowhood much that Melbourne had been in her girlhood; he flattered and courted her, she smiled graciously on him. He nicknamed her 'The Faery', a strange name for such a dumpy little woman, and laid flattery on, as he told Matthew Arnold, 'with a trowel'. She liked it. She liked his dash, his colourful character, and with stubborn characteristic inconsistency never managed even to be pleasant to his rival and successor, the serious, hard-working, high-minded, utterly Victorian Gladstone. Personality, as ever, came before politics with her.

Women nowadays would protest if her behaviour were described as characteristically feminine, in the sense that she was emotional, irrational, and over-dependent on the support and admiration of men, but it cannot be denied that, strong-willed though she was in many ways, she helped to perpetuate the view of 'the helpless little woman' who should not meddle in men's affairs. Her dislike of the growing Suffragette movement reinforced her public image of proper womanliness. She could have had an enormous impact on the position of women, if she had chosen, and would have found much support and enthusiasm from some of the greatest thinkers of the day. But she did not choose, and it is possible that her attitudes and behaviour retarded the cause of women's rights by decades.

Her final years, presiding over an enormously enlarged Empire, were glorious. She had outlived various patches of unpopularity, to become a symbol, almost an idol. The Diamond Jubilee of 1897, enormous and ostentatious, was the crowning glory of her long reign. In the previous ten years an area fifty times as large as Great Britain had been added to her dominions; the map of the world was covered with the pink-for-Britain patches that we can still see on old maps and in old geography books (see colour plate 5). This was the Empire on which, it was boasted, the sun never set. But the seeds of those troubles that were to ravage it during our own century were already planted, and Victoria's last years were clouded by the Boer War, a premonition of the conflicts that still rage in Africa. She died in 1901, at the end of an era, and that great scholar, G. M. Young, sums up her reign in this way:

> The Victorian age was over. The old queen was dead. She had lived long enough. The idol of her people, she had come to press on the springs of government with something of the weight of an idol, and in the innermost circle of public life the prevailing sentiment was relief.

Just as she had reacted against the manners of the Regency, so her son reacted against the long years he had spent under her shadow, and brought in a new style and a new age.

🔲🔲🔲🔲🔲🔲

THE MIDDLE CLASSES

🔲🔲🔲🔲🔲🔲

DURING this brief account of Victoria's influence, several references have been made to 'the new middle classes'. It is now time to look at them more closely. Where did they come from, how did they make their money, what were their tastes and attitudes? How did they differ from their predecessors?

In the eighteenth century, before the full impact of the Industrial Revolution, the pattern of life and the structure of society had been very different. Most of the population still lived in, and from, the country. The structure was basically feudal. The rich were the great landowners; the poor worked on the land. A few great families held all the power and guided the nation. England was still a rural rather than an industrial society. The story of the Industrial Revolution is outside the scope of this book, but the effect of the changes it caused belongs here, because it was not until Victoria's reign that these changes became widespread.

During Victoria's reign, Britain became immensely wealthy. Despite the extreme poverty of a large section of the community, the general standard of living rose; more people had better food and more material goods than ever before. The improvement was not confined to the old-established gentlefolk. Huge fortunes were made by the kind of people who had never had money before; it was not inherited money from estates, but money from trade and manufacturing. The new rich – or *nouveaux riches*, as we tend for some reason to label them – at the beginning of this period of expansion tended to be the railway barons, the owners of ironworks and steelworks, shipbuilders and canal builders, the engineers and developers of the new cities: as the century progressed, and the age of capitalism thrived, they were joined by bankers and financiers. The wealth came from the development of new processes and inventions, on a hitherto unknown scale, and as it grew, so did the population, though experts seem undecided as to whether population growth causes an increase in trade and wealth, or vice versa. Certainly the new factories needed hands to work in them; on the other hand, increased productivity could support an ever-growing number of people. Some of these workers were desperately poor, but on balance, historians seem to agree, they were little worse off than their predecessors who had laboured on the land. Bad harvests no longer brought ruin and starvation, except in Ireland, still a rural economy, where the potato famine starved millions to death. It is true that living conditions in the expanding cities were appalling, and dirt and overcrowding flourished; many of the Victorian slums we have inherited were actually built as part of reformed housing schemes, which gives one some idea of the squalor they must have replaced. Nevertheless, it was an age of great cities, and once the problems were recognized, immense efforts were made to tackle them. Society had become mobile rather than static, urban rather than peasant; some may have looked back with nostalgia to the golden age of cottage industry, but more rejoiced at new prospects. The proportion of people who grew rich through their own efforts undoubtedly multiplied enormously. New communications – railways, canals, steamships, daily papers – and new advertising techniques helped the flow of riches, both within the country and overseas. It was an age of undreamed-of growth and expansion. It created a new attitude to work, a new attitude to money, a new class system, a new society. It completely changed the expectations of vast masses of people.

Before this age, the educated upper classes did not expect to have to work for their money – or if they were obliged to work, they had to choose certain clearly defined professions. Younger sons who were not lucky enough to inherit an adequate income could become clergymen or lawyers, or they could enter the army or navy. (Medicine, which has since become such a respected and respectable profession, was then only on the borderline of acceptance, which was not surprising in view of the state of medical knowledge.) Women, of course, did not work at all; the very unfortunate could become teachers and governesses, but most went to great lengths to avoid this fate. Trade, in polite society, was something of a dirty word. There had of course for centuries been successful and enterprising traders, some of them of aristocratic origin, others self-made, and even the self-made could become, with the passage of time, thoroughly respectable. But they preferred to forget their ancestry, and to merge as quietly and discreetly as possible with the old-established country families, following old-established traditions of taste and behaviour. It was something of an effort to admit that a man could be 'in trade' and yet a gentleman, and to remind someone that his grandfather had been a grocer or a brewer could only be meant as an insult. The aristocratic ideal prevailed, even for those who could hardly afford it.

The novels of Jane Austen are a perfect guide for anyone interested in the finer shades of the pre-Victorian class spectrum. Few of her characters are from the upper ranks of the upper classes, although Mr Darcy in *Pride and Prejudice* owns a country house so grand that it is open to tourists, and Sir Walter Elliot in *Persuasion* is interested in nothing but titles and pedigree. But most of her characters are from the old middle classes; they have small estates, one or two sons are in the navy, one or two are clergymen. She also writes of farmers, governors, doctors and lawyers, who are allowed to mingle with their betters, as long as they remember their place. She seems certain that everybody has a place, though she is not so stupid as to assume that all well-born people are well-intentioned, or that all poor people are insensitive. She very much disliked the new spirit of commercial enterprise that was threatening to confuse the tidy, well-regulated familiar old world for ever, and which was to bring down the mighty and raise up the low. Her last, unfinished novel, *Sanditon*, is about commercial speculation; in it, she mocks both the energetic Mr Parker and the greedy Lady Denham who want to make money by developing quiet little Sanditon, and turning it into a thriving seaside resort. Already, we see the idea that making money is 'not quite nice'; it is more gentlemanlike, or ladylike, to live without display, genteelly, quietly, like the ladies in Mrs Gaskell's *Cranford*, with their 'elegant economy' and home-made jam. Inherited wealth is respectable (even when, like Sir Thomas Bertram's in *Mansfield Park*, it may well once have been associated with the slave trade); self-made wealth is not. There is more than a little of envy and sour grapes in this attitude; the old rich did not like to be overtaken by the new rich. They felt insecure. Mrs Gaskell's ladies cling to their gentility because it is all they have.

The new rich, on the other hand, were very keen to show off their new riches, and were not too worried by accusations of vulgarity. The Victorian age was an age of display, ostentation and magnificence, for those who could afford it. There was a violent reaction against the severe and somewhat uncomfortable elegance of design of the late eighteenth and early nineteenth century. Elegance had degenerated into austerity and timidity and mere plainness; the Victorians responded with an outburst of fantasy and creativity, unrestrained by fears of 'bad taste'. The Georgian drawing-room may have been more pleasing, by strict aesthetic standards, but the Victorian drawing-room, colourful, luxurious, confused, comfortable, overcrowded, is a paradise for the curious. The Victorians loved collecting, and crammed their houses with wax fruit and shells and fossils and butterflies and stuffed birds, with paisley shawls and papier-mâché trays, with plaster statues, and photographs and mementoes and souvenirs (see plate 13); they covered their walls with paintings, engravings, cards and mirrors; they covered their furniture with antimacassars and draperies; they filled every corner with screens and little tables and potted palms. They hated an empty space. The overall design was lost in a mass of fascinating detail. The Queen herself was no exception; she, too, was a collector, and never threw anything away. The house which she and Albert built for themselves on the Isle of Wight, Osborne, is still full of the clutter she

13. Bouquet of shell flowers made about 1845, probably at home.

accumulated (see plate 14). Leafing through photographs or
paintings of Victorian interiors, one is struck by the richness, the
variety, the colour, the oddity. There is no attempt at uniformity,
no concern for the clashing of styles. Look at the drawing-room
of Glen Roy, Moseley, Birmingham, a prosperous late Victorian
home (see plate 15); Nicholas Cooper in his book *The Opulent
Eye* says it is 'done up in historical styles that never were' – the
chimneypiece is 'Adams', the armoire on the right probably
French, and Japanese plum blossom is painted on the glass. We
are now far enough away from these fashions to see their charm.
These rooms must have been wonderfully exciting for everyone
except those who had to do the dusting. And, of course, there
were plenty of servants to do that.

14. The drawing-room at Osborne on the Isle of Wight.

For the new middle classes had more servants and lived on a scale more lavish than most of their socially superior, better-born country predecessors. No wonder clergymen on small incomes and unmarried daughters of small landowners shuddered when they saw the size of the competition. For those who did not opt out, the game of being middle class was becoming astonishingly expensive. In the old days, gentility had been enough in itself: James Austen Leigh, a wealthy nephew of Jane Austen, looks back with condescension to the times when ladies 'took a personal part in the higher branches of cooking. Some ladies liked to wash with their own hands the choice china after breakfast or tea.' He clearly finds this surprising, and hastens to reassure us that he was sure his own aunt had 'nothing to do with the mysteries of the stew-pot or the preserving pan' – though he is forced to admit that the silver and cutlery and furniture in her family home

15. The drawing-room at Glen Roy, Moseley, Birmingham: an example of the taste of a wealthy industrialist.

had been very plain, by modern standards (1871), and that it had been the fashion for gentlemen to carve their own meat at table! A servant of Jane Carlyle defined a proper lady as one 'who had not entered her own kitchen for seven years' – again, an ideal that would have been both expensive and difficult to maintain. The machinery of Victorian domestic life was, by preceding and succeeding standards, cumbersome, though it creaked on until world wars and washing machines brought it to a halt.

The new country houses built for the *nouveaux riches* are extraordinary monuments to a vanished life style. Plans show an amazing variety of rooms with different functions – smoking rooms, billiard rooms, luggage rooms, gun rooms, plate safes, linen rooms, work rooms, brushing rooms, still rooms, deed rooms, serveries, butler's pantries, not to mention morning rooms, drawing-rooms, picture galleries, libraries and bedrooms. Some were built in the style of medieval baronial halls, and decorated with suits of armour; others resembled gothic cathedrals or French châteaux. Merchants who had made their fortunes from commodities as varied as wool, cotton, beer, armaments, guano, china clay, and, in one case, ostrich feathers, acquired vast mansions and did their best to get their names into that catalogue of acceptability, *Burke's Landed Gentry*. The stories of these self-made men and their houses, gathered together by Mark Girouard in *The Victorian Country House*, are fascinating; one cannot but admire the enterprise of an industrialist like John Corbett (1817–1901) who started at the age of ten to work for his father in a small canal boat business, built up a fleet of his own boats, sold them before the railways killed the canals, and bought up the Stoke Prior Salt Works near Droitwich, which he turned into 'the most perfect system of salt manufacture in the world', with an annual output of 200,000 tons. On the proceeds, he built Château Impney, in the French style, an unexpected residence to find at Droitwich. Another very different kind of success was that of Lord Armstrong (1810–1900) who started life as a solicitor, but moved on to invent new types of hydraulic lifts and cranes, the Armstrong gun, and armour plating. His mansion, Cragside at Rothbury in Northumberland, was designed by Norman Shaw, and was the first in England, perhaps in the world, to be equipped, in 1880, with electric light. It is a vast romantic picturesque house, picturesquely situated on a steep slope, fitted, as Girouard says, for 'a modern war lord or robber baron' – yet over the dining fireplace is the homely inscription, 'East or West, Hame's Best'.

One of the most elaborate of these houses was Bear Wood (see plate 16), built by Kerr for John Walter, chief proprietor of *The Times*. It had its own gasworks, its own sawmills, its own water tower; it had twenty-two water closets and five bathrooms. It had interminable corridors, offices, and staircases, all with carefully differentiated functions. The design was ponderous; the

16. Bear Wood: a grandiose monument to architectural electicism.

entrance front, says Girouard, is like a sock in the jaw. Visitors to this mansion must often have been overawed – as, no doubt, they were intended to be. The thought of heating and cleaning such places is horrifying to us, with the present price of fuel and shortage of domestic servants, and it is somehow comforting to read that Walter could not maintain Bear Wood – *The Times* suffered from the challenge of the cheap press, and passed under Lord Northcliffe's control in 1908. The estate was sold up, and the house is now a school called Bearwood College.

The novels of Dickens contain some fine descriptions of vulgar show on a less enormous scale. The dinner party at the Veneerings' in *Our Mutual Friend* is a famous example. The Veneerings (their name is symbolic) are 'bran-new people in a bran-new house in a bran-new quarter of London . . . All their furniture was new, their plate was new, their carriage was new . . .' They also have a new coat of arms, a new fire escape, and a grand pianoforte with new action, and everything they so proudly own is highly polished and smells a little too much of the workshop. (A veneer is a superficial gloss or varnish, a thin layer often concealing an inferior article.) The Veneerings of course have plenty of useless servants, for show, but their most wonderful possession is an object that stands on the dining table; it represents a caravan of camels, and serves as a holder for fruit and flowers and candles, and even as a salt cellar, for some of the camels 'kneel down to be loaded with salt'. This astonishing table decoration was specially designed, we are told, for the Veneerings, when they were told by the Heralds' College that one of their ancestors had borne a camel on his shield, or might have done if he had thought of it. Dickens, of course, exaggerates, but many pieces of Victorian tableware and cutlery are as over-elaborate and eccentric as the camel salt cellar. They made fish knives too heavy and ornate to use (see plate 17), and épergnes so vast and so covered in curls and twirls that they must have proved very distracting to dinner guests, if the guests were lucky enough to be able to see each other round them (see plate 18). These objects were not designed for use but for show; art historians have pointed out that many of them look more like sacred items used for a religious ceremony than common household utensils. The home was the shrine, the dinner table the altar, the fish knives were sacrificial offerings.

17. Victorian fish servers, designed more for ornament than use.

18. An extreme example of Victorian table ornament: an épergne designed to commemorate Queen Victoria's Golden Jubilee in 1887.

Dickens found the new rich comic, but he was one of the new rich himself, and others in their turn laughed at him. When Jane Carlyle, wife of Thomas Carlyle, went to dinner with him she found the lavish display 'unbecoming to a literary man', and as she describes it, it has a touch of the Veneering vulgarity about it. 'The dinner,' she says, 'was served up in the new fashion – not placed on the table at all – but handed round –' (again, a sign that there was no shortage of servants) – 'only the dessert on the table and quantities of *artificial* flowers – but such an overloaded dessert! pyramids of figs, raisins and oranges – ach! . . the very candles rose each out of an artificial rose!' (1849). We could guess from this reaction that Jane Carlyle, a very lively letter writer and social historian, was herself of good family, but that she and her husband had known poverty and hard work. There may well be a touch of jealousy in her description; Dickens, though he, like Carlyle, was from a poor background, had 'made it' as a literary man, and was eager to show the world his success.

Not all objections to the new rich, however, were based on differences of taste and style. There was good reason to suspect the business morality of some of them, if not their domestic propriety. As Carlyle himself appreciated, huge fortunes were being made by employers who cared nothing for the living conditions of their workers, who treated human beings merely as 'paid hands', and who lived in luxury on the labour of others. In theory at least, the landowner of the old days had cared for his tenants and known them individually; the new factory owner had no connection with his men but the money he paid them – what Carlyle called 'the cash nexus'. The association of muck with money was both physical and moral: riches poured out of the filthy furnaces and smoke-belching factories of the North, and visitors who lived on the prosperity brought by iron, coal and steel recoiled with horror when they saw the industrial landscapes.

Victoria herself, visiting Manchester in 1852, was horrified by the dirt and smoke, and wrote in her Journal: 'As far as the eye can reach, one sees nothing but chimneys, flaming furnaces, many deserted but not pulled down, with wretched cottages around them . . . a thick and black atmosphere . . .' Disturbed by the memory, she commissioned William Wyld to paint a view of the city for her. He produced a landscape in which the factory chimneys are tactfully banished to the background, picturesque in the distance; in the foreground he placed a pretty country scene of vanishing rural England, with goats, cows and village maidens (see plate 19). The picture illustrates the understandable Victorian desire to keep the unpleasant at a safe distance, but it also reminds us that hideous though the cities were, there,

19. William Wyld's *Manchester from Kersal Moor*.

was as yet little suburban sprawl; Mrs Gaskell's characters can
walk out of the heart of Manchester to pick violets in the fields,
and when little Nell and her grandfather set off to escape from
London on foot, they are looking back in no time at the dome of
Saint Paul's from completely unspoilt countryside, according
to Cattermole's illustration (see plate 20).

'Where there's muck, there's money' is an old saying, and some
of Dickens' characters make money, literally, out of muck.
In *Our Mutual Friend* the Golden Dustman, Mr Boffin, makes his
living selling heaps of dust – coal dust, bone dust, vegetable dust,
crockery dust. Pip, in *Great Expectations*, is horrified when he
finds that the money he has inherited was not the gift of the mad
but aristocratic Miss Haversham, but the hard-earned gains of
the disgustingly uncouth old convict whom he had once befriended,
and who had worked for his riches as sheep farmer and stock
breeder and at other unnamed trades. Dickens has no simple
view of whether it is better to work hard for one's living as an

I.
Windsor Castle
in
Modern Times
by
E. W. Landseer.

2. *The Doubt: Can These Dry Bones Live?*
by H. A. Bowler.

ex-convict, or to live as a polite gentleman on other people's money. Like most of his generation he was in the process of working out a new attitude to work and gentlemanlike behaviour. The idea that unearned income is somehow wicked is fairly new, but one should remember that Friedrich Engels, who with Karl Marx was the father of communist thought, was working in his father's factory in Manchester during Victoria's visit. His classic study, *The Condition of the Working Class in England* published in 1845, was based on his observations of the labouring poor, and introduced the view that their sufferings would drive them forward to help themselves. The future, in his view, was theirs.

In *The Way We Live Now*, Anthony Trollope attacks the new world of financial speculation and greedy investors, and chooses railway mania for his subject. In the 1840s, Britain had gone mad with this new disease. Huge fortunes were made by those who

20. Cattermole's illustration from *The Old Curiosity Shop* of little Nell and her grandfather looking back at London.

bought shares in the ever-expanding network that covered Britain; George Hudson, the railway king who started work as a draper, was said to have made £100,000 in one day, and by 1844 had over a thousand miles of rail under his control. Unfortunately, the greed of the nation was so great that fraudulent companies were set up, many of which collapsed, ruining their shareholders, who were left with worthless railway 'scrip' instead of their life savings. Hudson himself, who had climbed to the height of social acceptability, as Lord Mayor of York, Member of Parliament for Sunderland, and friend of the great, was ruined when the Eastern Railway frauds were exposed. Trollope, in the character of Augustus Melmotte, a crooked financier, exposes the dishonesty of the speculator – and the creeping greed of the middle classes and the old impoverished aristocracy, who would accept anything from a man provided he was rich enough. Unfortunately, Trollope cannot resist making his most wicked characters foreign, as though unable to face the possibility that true-born Englishmen might prove as unscrupulous as crooks from other nations, but his portrait of money-crazed, idle England is far from flattering. Melmotte, incidentally, is rich on a very grand scale indeed; at one point in the novel he spends £10,000 on one banquet, a staggering sum in those days.

It is often said that the nineteenth century was the great age of capitalism. Capitalism is a word that we tend to use without much thought, but the nature of it can be brought home by a glance at documents of the period – for example, the prospectus of an intended joint stock company in 1854 advertises shares at £25 each; it requires capital of £120,000 for its project of supplying clean water to Newcastle, Gateshead and the Tyne Valley. This scheme, it tells prospective buyers, will not only be extremely profitable (like a similar scheme in Nottingham, which it quotes) – it will also be worthy and virtuous. By it, the working classes, very few of whom had running water in their homes at that period, will be spared much inconvenience and fatigue, as they will no longer have to walk with buckets to stand-pipes – and moreover, the prospectus adds, in a typical note of Victorian moralizing, this wonderful new scheme will also improve working class morals by preventing 'the promiscuous assemblages of young persons, while waiting for water at the places where it is sold'! What a glimpse we have here into a vanished way of life – the gatherings round the stand-pipe must have succeeded gatherings round the village pump, and the giggling and flirtations must have offended the eyes and ears of middle-class observers. Private enterprise offers the investor not only the hope of good profits on his money, but also the satisfaction of feeling good, by contributing to 'the comfort, cleanliness, sobriety and general morality of the working classes'. Such advertisements also remind us that many of the public services we now take for granted were then either non-existent, or run by private capital; we expect water provided by the water board or the local authority at the turn of a tap, but the Victorians had to rely on shareholders with a spare £25 to invest. Other services were fiercely competitive; the railway companies would vie with one another to offer the lowest fare between the same two places.

No wonder women were not supposed to interest themselves in this world of greed and dirt – though some, of course, did, and there is a story in Roebuck's *History of the Whigs* about an aristocrat married to an ironmaster, who shocks her ladylike relatives by her passionate interest in his profits – such interest is, they think, not nice. But the tables are turned when she declares the size of the profits – £300,000 in one year, she proudly announces. Her critics are silenced, though they cannot but wonder that such riches could be made 'all from that nasty cold iron'. Most women, however, did not meddle in their husbands' financial affairs. The Victorian age saw an increasing separation of male and female roles, of home and work. An ever-increasing crowd of middle-class men set off for work in the morning, leaving behind in their well-padded nests a generation of un-comprehending, under-employed, over-dressed wives. This separation helped the idolization of the home: the home became a sanctuary from the grim world of money and machinery, and the woman became 'The Angel in the House' – a phrase used as the title of a popular poem on married love by Coventry Patmore. Some women were satisfied with their role as decorative object and status symbol; others, particularly the unmarried like Florence Nightingale and Charlotte Brontë, were less happy.

Victorian dress for women was as impractical and over-decorated as Victorian fish knives (see plate 21). It reflected the same desire for display. Tight corsets and enormous crinolines, the most memorable fashion of the period, were for about ten years the daily wear of women who had nothing to do but issue orders to their servants, pay visits, play the piano, and add to the clutter of tapestry and embroidered bags and cushions with which they loved to fill their homes. Unfortunately, the vogue of the crinoline spread down the social scale, as fashions do, and was responsible for a good many accidents; it was hardly the ideal dress for women working in factories. Female boredom was common, and today we find it hard to imagine how our predecessors managed to occupy themselves until the master of the house came home. Charlotte Brontë, whose novels express a craving for a more adventurous life, complains in *Jane Eyre* of a life of knitting stockings and embroidering bags. One can guess that she disliked sewing herself, because her heroines tend to prick their fingers so much while doing it – yet even Charlotte sewed, and Haworth Parsonage displays some of the things she made during the long dull evenings, when she had no company but her ageing father. In Arnold Bennett's novel *The Old Wives' Tale* there is a fine picture of female rebelliousness; in the first chapter, Constance and Sophia Baines sit in the window above their father's shop, pressing their noses against the glass in an unladylike way as they watch their servant, Maggie, meeting her boyfriend – or 'follower', as the admirers of servants were called. They are bored. The good sister, Constance, is making a tapestry firescreen for her mother's birthday, with ugly mustard-tinted wool: Bennett mocks the design, but says that the girl's grace 'excused and invested with charm an activity which, on artistic grounds, could not possibly be justified'. So must many Victorian men have felt, as they watched their womenfolk embarking on yet another piece of useless decoration.

Of course, not all the objects made were ugly; some are now collectors' pieces. The range of activity was as large as the space

21. An illustration from a fashion magazine of 1860.

it had to fill. Seaweed albums and pictures, boxes decorated with pine cones and feathers and shells, carefully dressed dolls and pressed flower arrangements bear witness to hours of work, some of it no doubt satisfying enough. *The Ladies' Magazine* of 1850 tells us that 'Elegant Arts for Ladies comprise the making of Feather Flowers, Hair Ornaments, Porcupine Quill Work,

Printing on Vellum, Velvet and Glass, Gilt Leatherwork, the Gilding of Plaster Casts, Bead and Bugle Work, Seaweed Pictures and the mysteries of Diaphanie and Potichomanie' – enough to keep any young lady out of harm's way. Whoever made the shell book of seaweeds illustrated in the *Lady's Newspaper* (10 March 1852) had good reason to feel pleased with herself. It is charming (see plate 22).

Another pastime consisted of quarrelling with the servants. Many women had not been brought up, as had the members of the old gentry, to 'manage' a large household of servants, and *Punch* of the period is full of cartoons illustrating 'Servant-galism' – the struggles of the mistress of the house to impose her will on stupid or strong-willed cooks, maids or footmen (see plate 23a). Such struggles must have absorbed a good deal of surplus energy, and induced many a Victorian migraine.

There are plenty of jokes about the crinoline in *Punch*, too, which come as a relief; at least the Victorians themselves noticed the absurd nature of this ridiculous garment (see plate 23b). Apart from the physical inconvenience, imagine the unnecessary yards and yards of expensive material that went into each one, a sure sign of an affluent society. Others protested against the habit of tight lacing and the vogue for the unnaturally tiny waist, which permanently deformed the rib cages of countless

22. A shell book of seaweeds as illustrated in *The Lady's Newspaper*, 1852.
(Reproduced from an original copy of the newspaper.)

23. Two Leech cartoons from *Punch*, about 1858.

(A) SERVANTGALISM. *Lady.* 'Wish to leave! Why Thompson, I thought you were very comfortable with me?'

Thompson (who is extremely refined). 'Hoh, yes, ma'am, I don't find no fault with you, ma'am. But the truth is, ma'am, the hother servants is so 'orrid vulgar, and hignorant, and speaks so hungrammatical, that I reely can't live in the same 'ouse with them!'

(B) CRINOLINE ON THE WATER. *Waterman.* 'You've no call to be afeard, Miss; we're licensed to carry six!'

girls, and which outlasted the crinoline; the crinoline, at its most grotesque in the 1860s, had disappeared by 1870. The painter G. F. Watts published an article 'On Taste in Dress' in 1883, in which he complained that corsets were unhealthy and unnatural, and that a tiny waist was not necessarily beautiful; in response he received a letter from a lady called Gertie Tippla who wrote:

> 'Dear Sir,
>
> A party of girls here in Norwood are trying to get up a society calling itself the Anti-Tight Lacing Society, we have had some meetings etc., but much wish to have a president who will fully sympathise with our object – namely that of showing girls and others round us how wicked and ugly the fashion of tight lacing is . . . '

Watts became president, but tiny waists remained the ideal until the First World War, which forced on both sexes a more realistic attitude to women, work and dress.

So there they are, the men and women of the new middle classes: the men hard-working and ambitious, the women idle and occasionally dissatisfied. In many ways they were supremely confident, as they carved their way through mountainsides, built suspension bridges over enormous valleys, planned underground railways, defied nature by bringing a ship canal thirty-five miles inland into the heart of Manchester. No feats of engineering were too great for them to contemplate. Their visions were grandiose, their monuments immense. They produced explorers and missionaries of both sexes, who travelled round the world, some for profit, some with ostensibly higher motives, building up and expanding the Empire and naval command that had been founded centuries earlier; the last half of Victoria's reign witnessed an amazing growth of British territory (see colour plate 5). The Victorians believed more deeply than we, in a more troubled and less prosperous age can imagine, that 'Britain was Best'. The growth of empire was a symbol of their confidence; they genuinely believed that the poorer nations of India and Africa would profit not only from our engineering and railroads, but also from our culture, religion and legal institutions. And to some extent they did. But nowadays we are conscious of the wrongs done to other nations by British greed and arrogance, and admit responsibility for the extermination of traditional ways of life, indeed of whole races; but in the nineteenth century such questions were raised only by the most far-sighted and humane of travellers.

The life and adventures of David Livingstone provide a fine example of the virtues and limitations of the Victorian spirit. Born into a large, poor, hard-working family, he started work in the mills as a child, and educated himself in the evenings; he set his heart upon becoming a missionary, overcame all the obstacles of his background, and made his way to Africa, where he preached the British virtues of hard work, thrift, punctuality, personal ambition and monogamy to African tribesmen who saw these things as vices to be avoided. He seems to have been harsh and callous to his own wife, and indifferent to the sufferings of his children, whom he dragged with him on various travels before dispatching them back to a hard and lonely life in England. He was in some ways a classic hypocrite: he condemned drink for the poorer classes, but saw no harm in private drinking for the well-to-do. Public abstinence was useful only as an example. Yet despite these contradictions, he was inspired by a genuine hatred of the slave trade, which had been abolished in the British Empire in 1833, but flourished elsewhere, ignored by Spain, France and Portugal, and actively pursued by the Arabs and some Africans, who were eager to sell their fellows into captivity for gain. Livingstone saw that legitimate commerce could replace the slave trade, and provide Africans with a means of buying European goods; commerce and trade, as so often in the nineteenth century, were thus elevated to an almost religious significance. Commerce and Christianity, hand in hand, would bring peace and civilization to Africa. Enlightened self-interest would be good for both parties. This pragmatic approach worked well, and British influence in Africa prospered, though it must be admitted that Livingstone's success at converting the heathen was negligible. But he was more patient and understanding than some of his fellow missionaries, and less bigoted on the subject of polygamy and tribal customs. And his mission was, after all, a glorious success in the eyes of the world; he may not have christened many Africans, but he had the great satisfaction of christening Lake Victoria, Lake Albert and the Victoria Falls.

Livingstone was a man of outstanding perseverance and courage, but the Empire also provided a useful overspill for many less famous and more questionable characters who did not fit easily into the constricting British framework. Convicts were transported, most of them to Australia's Botany Bay, some to the West Indies; others went voluntarily. Younger sons who got into scrapes could disappear into India, to prosper or perish. Enterprising spinsters such as Charlotte Brontë's friend, Mary Taylor, could make a new life in New Zealand, where it was not undignified for a woman to open a shop, as she did, and where there was a plentiful supply of unmarried men. Some emigrated reluctantly, forced from home by unemployment; Ford Madox Brown's painting *The Last of England* (see colour plate 4), painted to celebrate the departure of Brown's sculptor friend, Thomas Woolner, for Australia, portrays a certain mixture of feelings – the 'honest family of the greengrocer type' look more hurt and anxious than joyfully expectant, and behind them, again in Brown's own words, 'a reprobate shakes his fist with curses at the land of his birth'. The glories of expansion had their darker side. (Woolner stayed only two years, from 1852–4, in Australia; his attempts at gold prospecting were not a success!)

In recent years, as the countries which Britain ruled have gained independence, there has been much re-appraisal of the British role overseas. Were we overbearing, insensitive, greedy and exploiting, or did we, as we claimed, export ideals of democracy and justice in exchange for cheap food? The history of India, so long interwoven with our own, is a fascinating illustration of the complexities of national interchange. There are many alive today who remember the British Raj with affection, and India has adopted for herself many of the political and judicial procedures introduced in the days of empire; on the other hand, many writers have written scathing portraits of ignorant, petty British officials. Even Kipling, long considered an Imperialist in spirit, is now seen to be more critical of the system than his contemporaries supposed, and E. M. Forster's *A Passage to India* is a devastating condemnation of our insularity and prejudice that lingered on, fatally, well into the twentieth century. Behind the happy reminiscences of old colonels lies a long history of outrage. The Indian Mutiny of 1857, in which many innocent European women and children were massacred, left a terrible scar on Anglo-Indian relations; the massacres were horrible, but so were the reprisals, and hundreds of mutineers were hacked to pieces, blown from cannon, and publicly hanged, while British officers looked on and sipped their whisky and soda. Patriotism at home ran high; it says a good deal for the common sense and conciliatory spirit of Victoria that the outcome was not even bloodier. She, with unusual political insight, proclaimed a policy of 'generosity, benevolence and religious toleration', and declared that 'the deep attachment which her Majesty feels to her own religion and the comfort and happiness she derives from its consolations will preclude her from any attempt to interfere with the native religions' – a remarkably advanced view for the time, and for such an emotional moment in that time. Thanks partly to her sense of responsibility, the British were able to continue to enjoy their mango chutney and cups of tea, their curry and kedgeree, their polo and their gymkhanas, with the result that many Indian words and customs have become part of everyday English life. Cultural exchange with India was a genuine two-way process, though many Victorians may not have recognized this fact at the time.

It is not surprising that the British felt superior to the more primitive races they conquered, such as the Australian Aboriginals, whose skills they were unable to recognize. More surprising is the way in which their patriotism and complacency led them to condescend to other advanced European nations, and to newly-independent America. Visitors from abroad commented on the insularity of attitude they found here, and we of course, saw it not as a defect but as a virtue. Ralph Waldo Emerson, in his entertaining account of the English, *English Traits*, tells this story: 'An English lady in the Rhine hearing a German speaking of her party as foreigners, exclaimed, "No, we are not foreigners; we are English; it is you that are foreigners."' He describes the English belief that they are the centre of the modern world (and agrees with it); finds their patriotism 'childish'; is amused by the fact that 'Mr Coleridge is said to have given public thanks to God, at the close of a lecture, that he had defended him from being able to utter a single sentence in the French language.' Americans in English fiction tend to appear as money-making speculators, lively divorcees, or match-making heiresses eager to catch a duke; the occasional outspoken feminist also appears.

> Delia Dodds, the lecturer from 'the States',
> Upon the Woman's Question

referred to in Mrs Browning's poem *Aurora Leigh* sounds like an ancestor of Betty Friedan and Kate Millett, modern feminists, and also foreshadows the independent globe-trotting American women journalists who appear in the novels of American-born Henry James later in the century, characters viewed with mingled fear and admiration. There were some colourful, real-life American characters to be met in Britain; an archetypal figure was Robert Cumming Schenck, who was appointed Minister to Great Britain in 1871, and created a stir by introducing draw poker, a game for which he had a passion. In 1876 he resigned under a cloud, having committed the diplomatic sin of allowing his name to be used in the purchase of stock in a silver mine called Emma in Utah. Silver mines and poker – how different from our own aristocratic ambassadors!

There were of course many Americans who presented a different image, in their writings and in their visits. Emerson himself was warmly received by Carlyle, by Wordsworth, and by the many institutes here who invited him over to lecture. Harriet Beecher Stowe toured Britain in triumph after the publication of *Uncle Tom's Cabin*, which was a best seller here; her success was comparable to that of Dickens in America. Children in both continents devoured the works of Louisa M. Alcott, whose *Little Women* and *Good Wives*, despite a background of Civil

War, present a picture of American home life which is far removed from frontier violence, and with which English children today still feel a sense of kinship and familiarity. Tennyson admired Edgar Allen Poe, who in turn admired Elizabeth Barrett Browning, and dedicated a volume of his poetry to her. Longfellow's poems were widely read here; the *Wreck of the Schooner Hesperus* and *The Village Blacksmith* were sung at many an English musical evening, and a dying soldier at Sebastopol quoted the popular *Psalm of Life* with his last breath. The Brownings met Margaret Fuller, the American feminist, in Italy; 'Dear, brave, noble Margaret Fuller', Robert described her, and both admired her work for the emancipation of both slaves and women.

An American man of letters like Charles Eliot Norton had friends on both sides of the Atlantic; he knew Carlyle, Mrs Gaskell, Ruskin, Rossetti and Clough in England, Lowell and Emerson in the States, and was related to half the distinguished Bostonians of his time. He was widely read and widely travelled in Europe and the East; his art lectures at Harvard, and his contributions to the *Atlantic Monthly*, the *North American Review* and the *Nation* (of which he was a founder) had an immense effect on his own country's cultural development. He was a living contradiction of the popular picture of the American wild frontiersman.

So the gulf of understanding was not impassable. Mutual friendships between the nations could and did flourish, but only perhaps for the enlightened, for those who could read and travel. To the average Englishman, Europe was clever and corrupt, and America a frightening and lawless wilderness, where money ruled and morality kept quiet – attitudes that linger on today, encouraged by movies and television. There was some truth in the English picture of America; life there was less safe and orderly, less comfortable, except in the oldest established states. The English were alarmed and fascinated by Mark Twain's irreverent mocking of European culture, by James Fenimore Cooper's picture of the harsh struggles of pioneers and trappers in novels like *The Last of the Mohicans*. From their safe little island, the English watched with mingled sympathy, horror and envy as America hacked its way through Indian territory, rushed west for gold, struggled through the Civil War, and tried to accommodate the varied tides of immigrants that came her way in search of fortune and freedom. No wonder that in this country we felt complacent; our naval power was the greatest in the world, our industry the most prosperous. We could afford to look down on other races and their misfortunes. It seems rather foolish now to look at England as the geographical centre of the world, but it did not seem foolish to the Victorians, any more than the Romans thought it foolish to regard Rome as the city to which all roads should lead.

Yet this immense certainty generated its moments of doubt. The industrial magnates and empire builders felt superior to other nations, but at home they were often insecure, confused by rapid change, eager to learn the rules of polite society. They employed governesses to teach their daughters the manners and accents they could not provide at home; they sent their sons off to the new public schools to learn the same skills. It was an age of transition, as Albert, more responsive to the needs of the nation than his Queen, was quick to appreciate. It was partly to establish the confidence and celebrate the achievements of this rapidly developing, thrusting, complex new society that Albert, in a moment of inspiration, conceived the idea of the Great Exhibition of 1851, one of the earliest international exhibitions ever held. It was such an important event in the history of the development of Victorian taste and consciousness that it deserves a section to itself. The novelist Thomas Hardy was to call it 'a precipice in time', and we have records of the deep impression it made on many contemporary observers. It sums up the spirit of boundless energy and optimism of the age.

THE GREAT EXHIBITION

THE Great Exhibition was an exhibition of science and manufacture, of design and raw materials, unprecedented in aim and achievement. Even the building which housed it, happily labelled The Crystal Palace by *Punch*, was a triumph of imaginative architecture (see plate 24). Designed by Joseph Paxton, after the model of the Great Conservatory at Chatsworth, it soared up, a glittering canopy of glass and steel; Lord Macaulay who was present at the opening came away enraptured, and wrote that it was 'a most gorgeous sight; vast; graceful; beyond the dreams of the Arabian romance. I cannot think that the Caesars ever exhibited a more splendid spectacle. I was quite dazzled . . .'

The reference to the Caesars is revealing, for the Victorians showed a Roman determination to overcome obstacles. One of the objections to the building of the Palace in Hyde Park was that it would involve cutting down a clump of three tall elms on the site – the Victorians, too, could show concern for conservation, when it suited them. So Paxton incorporated the trees in his design, and an immense transept was built to house them. They must have added to the exotic, fairy tale quality of the place. Paxton's whole concept was in fact based on nature; he is thought to have devised the rib structure from his study of the huge South American water lily, *Victoria Regina*, which he had seen at Chatsworth; its giant leaves were strong enough to bear the weight of Paxton's small daughter. Like so many of the great Victorians, Paxton was strictly an amateur, as he had no professional qualifications as architect, engineer or scientist;

24. The Crystal Palace, home of the Great Exhibition.

this was an age when the inspired amateur, his imagination unshackled by a narrow professional training or discipline, could achieve astonishing results.

The elms were not the only excuse for opposition to Albert's scheme. Some muttered that it would ruin Hyde Park, the only decent open space left in London; others feared the building, unorthodox by any standards, would collapse. A more natural fear, perhaps, was that the huge crowds it would attract might prove violent, and that it might provide an opportunity for a rekindling of the radical spirit of Chartism which had inflamed the working classes in the previous decade. The Victorians were easily alarmed by the idea of a 'mob', and memories of the French Revolution lingered; more recently, Revolution had swept through Europe in 1848, and the English feared that it might be their turn next. The discontent of a badly-paid, badly-housed proletariat could not be totally ignored many felt, though that was not how they expressed their alarm. 'I would advise those living near the Park to keep a sharp look over their silver forks and spoons and servant maids,' wrote one angry colonel to

3. The interior of the saloon carriage of Queen Victoria's royal train, which can still be seen in the National Railway Museum, York.

4. *The Last of England* by Ford Madox Brown.

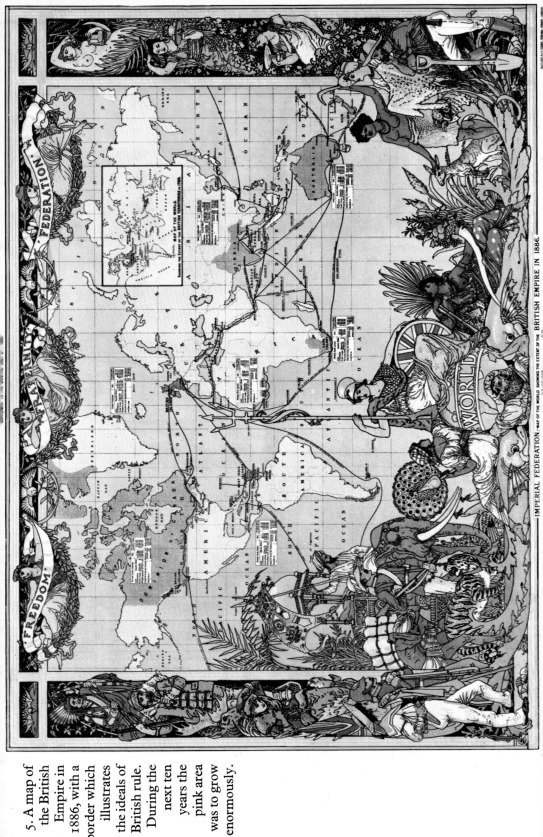

IMPERIAL FEDERATION — MAP OF THE WORLD SHOWING THE EXTENT OF THE BRITISH EMPIRE IN 1886.

5. A map of the British Empire in 1886, with a border which illustrates the ideals of British rule. During the next ten years the pink area was to grow enormously.

The Times. But his fears were unfounded. The crowds were orderly and loyal, nobody took advantage of the situation to attempt to assassinate or even to shout abuse at Queen Victoria, and there was no drunken vandalism – perhaps wisely, the refreshments available did not include alcoholic beverages. The exhibits, ranging in scale from meat-paste pot lids to huge power looms, were generally considered wonderful, and the whole project, which had been financed entirely by private money, made a large profit.

But was it an artistic success? Did it not, rather, illustrate what we think of as typically Victorian 'bad taste'? One could argue either way. Sir Nikolaus Pevsner, an expert on design, writes: 'The attendance as well as the size of the buildings and the quantity of the products shown was colossal. The aesthetic quality of the products was abominable.' These are hard words. He goes on to argue that designers had not yet learned to cope with the newly invented processes of production, such as machine weaving and electro-plating, and were applying the wrong techniques to the wrong materials. Certainly some of the objects indicate more pride in the fact that a thing *can* be done than interest in the use or beauty of the finished object – take, for example, the wonderful knife with eighty blades and other instruments, made by Rodgers and Sons of Sheffield (see plate 25). It was heavily decorated with gold inlay, etching and engraving – a remarkable piece of work, but neither use nor ornament. The Osler fountain of cut crystal glass was famed more for its size and weight than for its beauty; it weighed four tons (see plate 26). Designs for carpets and fabrics show, as Pevsner points out, a lack of restraint, a lack of plan, a picking from here and there of jumbled scraps of pattern, a confused eclecticism. Eclecticism is a word one cannot avoid long when talking of the Victorians, for it so perfectly describes their attitude to decoration; it is the art of borrowing from various sources, to suit oneself. The Victorians had a great deal to be eclectic about; easier travel and the spreading Empire, as well as new techniques, provided a vast range of new patterns – peacocks from India, carpet designs from Turkey and Persia, lace designs from France, even sphinxes

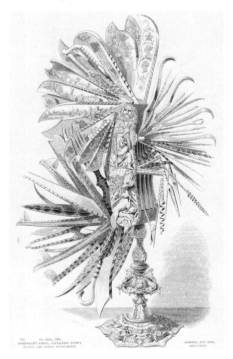

25. The eighty-bladed knife, exhibited by Rodgers & Sons, Sheffield.

from Egypt. The Victorian instinct was not to look for uniformity of style, but to jumble everything up together, at random; even a room like The Indian Room at 7 Chesterfield Gardens, which at first sight looks as though it is trying to keep to some kind of Far Eastern plan, proves on closer inspection to combine Indian, Japanese, Chinese, and European bamboo chairs (see plate 27). Most interiors had even less coherence, and individual designs could show several separate influences.

So the Great Exhibition had, in the world of art, an immensely useful function; it drew attention to the chaos of taste and to the evils of 'Sheffield Eternal' and 'Brummagem Gothic'. From this chaos emerged art critics such as Ruskin, and designers and artists such as William Morris. The artistic directors who had helped to set up the exhibition had already declared their desire for reform; Henry Cole and Owen Jones felt that 'ornament must

26. The celebrated Osler cut-crystal fountain.

be secondary to the thing ornamented', and that ornament should be fitted to the object's function. The Exhibition proved a focus for their theories and a breeding ground for new theories, as well as a display of the dangers and disasters of the age. Some of the new ideas were of course already in the air – the architect Augustus Welby Pugin was in charge of the medieval court, where he had scope to exhibit his highly original and influential views on design. He was of the opinion that

> All the mechanical contrivances and inventions of the day, such as plastering, composition, papier-mâché, and a host of other deceptions, only serve to degrade design, by abolishing the variety of ornament and ideas, as well as the boldness of execution, so admirable and beautiful in ancient carved works . . .

27. The Indian room at 7, Chesterfield Gardens, London.

We see here the growing revulsion against the new machine age of mass production and cheap imitation materials, and a new interest in the old arts of craftsmanship. (Today, some feel the same revulsion from plastic, nylon, and other 'unnatural' materials.) Professional designers were almost unknown in the early Victorian period; in the later half of the century, they were to flourish.

But the Great Exhibition offered far more than a spectacle of bad taste. Many of its visitors saw their first railway train there, and machinery of most kinds was still a novelty. A model diving bell, a lace machine, and a steam brewery attracted great attention. The Victorians may have liked over-decoration in luxury goods, but they had a strong sense of functional design; the sewing machine (see plate 28), the typewriter, the earthenware

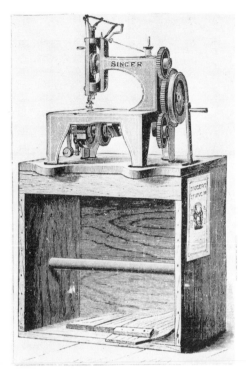

28. Victorian functional design: an early Singer sewing machine.

inhaler, and the gynaecological forceps remained unchanged for many years after their original conception. British engineering was the best in the world, encouraged by the efforts of men like James Nasmyth, the inventor of the steam hammer, and his pupil Joseph Whitworth, whose machine tools at the Great Exhibition were praised for 'their great beauty and power'. The nineteenth-century toolmakers have been acclaimed by modern art historians as a new race of artists, and even at the time, objects like lathes and microscopes were considered beautiful as well as useful; more significantly, many appreciated that they were beautiful because they were useful. The English, said Emerson, love 'the lever, the screw and the pulley', and as early as 1759 the economist Adam Smith had stated that 'Utility is one of the principle sources of beauty.'

Over-decoration and embellishment never overwhelmed such inventions as the bicycle and the electric light bulb – the shape of the light bulb is so well adapted to its function that we accept it, says Herwin Schaefer in an excellent account of the functional tradition, 'as if it were a product of nature'. Significantly, more attempts were made to decorate the sewing machine and the typewriter, because they were primarily used by women, but even here the dignity of the basic design survived. Schaefer advises us, when looking for a good design, to concentrate not on luxury items such as the Osler fountain, but on ordinary objects in daily use, such as egg beaters, kitchen scales, scissors and coat hooks, bottles, pots and bell pushes. It is interesting to note that the American exhibits that most impressed the British were such things as sleighs, ice skates, racing sulkies, canoes and farm implements; necessity was proving the mother of invention and by the 1870s the Americans had taken over the world lead in machinery, as they demonstrated in 1876 at the Centennial Exhibiton in Philadelphia.

The nineteenth-century conflict between function and decoration was nowhere better expressed than in the building of the railways. The telling contrast between the elaborate Gothic façade of St Pancras, more a cathedral than a railway terminus, and the austere simplicity of the roof and girders within is still eloquent (see plate 29). The Victorians themselves were conscious of such problems, and in 1852 Frederick S. Williams published a book, *Our Iron Roads*, which shows a spirited enthusiasm for the immense enterprise of the engineers, and for the beauty of their constructions. The railways have retained their excitement and glamour for some addicts, and Williams is one of their earlier admirers. Of the High Level Bridge at Newcastle, he writes:

> It is scarcely possible to imagine a more interesting and beautiful sight than it presents, with the huge span of arches diminishing in perspective, and the opening at the furthest end of the bridge showing only like a bright spot in the distance. The pillars, which carry the road, add greatly to the picturesque effect . . . such a combination of beautiful lines is seldom seen. (See plate 30.)

29. Paddington Station in 1854. Like St Pancras, a fine example of the beauty of engineering design.

30. The High Level Bridge at Newcastle-upon-Tyne.

Here is a writer who does not despise the machine-made. He writes with equal lyricism of the Britannia tubular bridge across the Menai Strait:

> Could the reader stand upon the shores of the Isle of Anglesey, and view the entire spectacle, though but for a few moments, on some fine spring evening, he would retire with impressions of its magnificence that neither pen nor pencil can create . . . Science and nature mingle in harmonious contrast, and receive the grateful homage of every rightly-constituted heart.

Williams clearly did not share the fears of Wordsworth, who thought that the railways would ruin the scenery of the Lake District.

He is also impressed by sheer technical triumphs, such as the blasting of a tunnel through Shakespeare's Cliff between Dover and Folkestone, an event which attracted crowds of admiring sightseers, at the risk of their lives. It has been suggested that the fiery and dramatic paintings of John Martin, now restored to fashion after years of neglect, may have been partly inspired by the sight of the quarries and craters and scars that gashed Britain during the building of the railways; he was very fond of portraying caverns, tunnels, and falling rocks. His versions of Hell remind one of the fiery furnaces of industrial England, and his huge work, *Belshazzar's Feast*, distinctly resembles a vast railway station (see colour plate 6). Martin certainly appreciated the picturesque aspects of engineering feats, as well as their practical ones – significantly, he devoted a good deal of time not only to Biblical and classical subjects, but also to designing and drawing schemes for sewage and water supplies, embankments and colliery safety apparatus. Most Victorians were, like him, moved rather than appalled by the grandeur of the new engineering miracles, and Londoners watched the new cuttings slicing their way into the heart of the city with awe.

Yet efforts were made to landscape the railways; Williams had strong views on appropriate designs for tunnels and bridges. Tunnel entrances, he says, should show 'plainness combined with boldness, and massiveness without heaviness', which sounds sensible enough. But his book has illustrations which prove how difficult it was for the Victorians to find appropriate designs for wholly new concepts – there is a railway station that looks like a gothic chapel, a tunnel entrance with castellated towers modelled on a medieval castle (see plate 31), and the Britannia bridge, a triumph of modern engineering, was flanked by highly inappropriate sphinxes. Eclecticism at work, again. The bridges themselves dictated their own aesthetic laws, but when it came to decorating them, and blending them in with traditional ideas of the beautiful, the Victorians were less happy, and had less to guide them.

31. Shugborough Tunnel.

The Great Exhibition, which provided an opportunity for much debate on design, also created a new attitude to work, which was to prove equally significant. Work had become respectable; trade and manufacture were given the nation's blessing. Albert himself, who could have chosen to be little more than an idle and handsome figurehead, was much inspired by the romance of industry, and worked hard himself, contributing to the view that hard work is good even for the richest of us. In the words of *The Economist* of 1851, 'Labour is ceased to be looked down upon . . . the Bees are more considered than the Butterflies of society; wealth is valued less as an exemption from toil, than as a call to effort . . .' The idea of a leisured class of wealthy parasites became less popular, as the work ethic and the virtues of self help took over. Sir Felix Carbury in Trollope's *The Way We Live Now* is shown as even more contemptible than the unscrupulous Melmotte, because, although well-born, he is a complete idler and wastrel, who does nothing but play cards, hunt, borrow money, seduce poor girls, and plot to marry rich ones. The polite world of Jane Austen, in which families lived without visible means of support, was on the way out. Religion placed itself firmly on the side of the worker; God would help those who helped themselves. Samuel Smiles published in 1859 a book called *Self Help*, which became the Bible of the self-made man; he also published glowing biographies of men like George Stephenson, and praised the great industrialists who had started from humble origins.

Commerce had become respectable, and great buildings rose to celebrate the civic pride of the great commercial centres – Cuthbert Brodrick's Town Hall in Leeds (see plate 32), Bunning's Coal Exchange in London, Edward Walters' Free Trade Hall in Manchester. These, one could say, were the real cathedrals of Victorian England. Ruskin and Pugin were to look back nostalgically at the gothic cathedrals of a more spiritual age, but they could not stem the flow of pride in profit, in invention, in commercial daring. The Crystal Palace glorified the golden age of prosperity. In the official catalogue, Albert wrote 'We are living at a period of most wonderful transition', and went on to

32. Leeds Town Hall.

sing the praises of a unified world, in which 'thought is communicated with the rapidity and even by the power of lightning'. Science, industry and art together will, he said, help us to fulfil the sacred mission of man, helped on by the stimulus of competition and capital. Endless progress, sings *The Economist*, in a fine confident moment, is 'the destined lot of the human race'. And England was firmly in the forefront of that progress, a model to the world.

It is pleasing to note that the profits raised from the Great Exhibition went into educational projects which we can still enjoy today; again, the vision was Albert's, and the projects include the Victoria and Albert Museum, the Natural History Museum, and the Royal College of Music. Triumphant commerce did not neglect succeeding generations.

ꕥꕥꕥꕥꕥ

THE OTHER NATION

ꕥꕥꕥꕥꕥ

FROM the triumphs of Victorian England, we must turn to the
darker side. This great age of progress also contained suffering
and poverty almost too painful to recall. The prosperous and the
genteel turned their eyes away from the dirty, immoral, ill-
mannered poor, and shut their doors firmly behind them. Some
maintained that the poor were poor through their own fault,
believing, against all the evidence, that all who wanted to help
themselves and better themselves could do so. Others asserted
that unemployment and poverty were necessary to stimulate
competition and keep wages low. Others were interested only in
their own profits, and simply did not care about the workers,
treating them as creatures from another race. Terrible hardships
were accepted as commonplace. A kind man like Charles Lamb
proved so insensitive to the misery of boy chimney-sweeps that
in his essay *In Praise of Chimney Sweepers* he writes with un-
comprehending condescension of

> these young Africans of our own growth – these almost clergy imps,
> who sport their cloth without assumption; and from their little
> pulpits (the tops of chimneys), in the nipping air of a December
> morning, preach a lesson of patience to mankind.

He does not improve our opinion of him when he goes on to say:

> Reader, if thou meetest one of these small gentry in thy early rambles,
> it is good to give him a penny – it is better to give him twopence.

Well-intentioned he may be, but he seems quite unaware of the
fact that many of these imps met horrible deaths in chimney

flues and that all of them led a life of intolerable misery and danger.

Luckily others, less complacent, were outraged. Lord Shaftsbury agitated for acts to restrict working hours and improve working conditions for women and children, and in 1863 Charles Kingsley published *The Water Babies*, which forced people to see the plight of the sweeps in a new light. But it was slow work; it took Shaftsbury thirty years of effort to protect these children by law. Once the conscience of the country had been aroused, commissions and select committees were set up; hundreds of hard-working officials and laymen whose names are now forgotten investigated labour, sanitation, health and housing, and published their shocking findings in reports and Parliamentary Papers. These reports were known as Blue Books, from the colour of their bindings, and were first made available to the public in 1836; some Victorians, including Dickens, mocked the Blue Book, statistic-collecting mentality, which they saw as the foundation of a dull, interfering, unimaginative bureaucracy. But these reports make gripping and horrifying reading, and one must feel the greatest admiration for those who patiently compiled them. The size of the problem, due to population increase, the rapid growth of industrialization and the shift to the cities, was enormous; luckily there were some brave enough to tackle it.

Perhaps the most appalling of these matters is, to us, the question of child labour. The middle-class Victorians idealized children and family life, delighting, as we have seen, in such portraits as Millais's *Bubbles*; how could these same people have allowed boys of seven to die in chimneys, girls of eight to pull trucks in mines, children of three and four to pick up cotton waste, creeping under dangerous unguarded machines in textile factories, where bigger people could not go? (See plate 33.) The age that idolized maternity in poems and paintings, in real life sent mothers back down the mines so soon after childbirth that they would take their children down with them – 'even children of six years of age do much to relieve the burden', writes one witness. The conditions in which these children worked were shocking:

Chained, belted and harnessed like dogs in a go-cart, black, saturated with wet, and more than half naked, crawling upon their hands and feet, and dragging their loads behind them – they present an appearance indescribably disgusting and unnatural.

protests a commissioner in the Mines Report of 1842.

33. *Love Conquers Fear*, a factory scene in 1839.

Nor were workers above ground much luckier. A girl who worked in an ivory, pearl and tortoise-shell cutting factory in Sheffield, producing useless luxury articles such as the Rodgers 80-bladed knife, working at least a fourteen-hour day, often more, comments with seeming carelessness:

> I have been very careful about machines ever since a girl of nine or ten years old. We girls in some works of this kind were playing at hiding, and one about fourteen years old hid beside a drum in a wheel not then working, and it was started and crushed her to pieces. They had to pick her bones up in a basket, and that's how they buried her . . . girls are soft, giddy things . . . (1865).

One may suspect a touch of Dickensian exaggeration in the description of the bones in the basket, for the Victorians delighted in horror stories, but it remains a fact that the accident rate in factories was appallingly high, so high that minor accidents were not even considered: one employer in a paper mill writes nonchalantly of his young workers: 'They seem to cut their fingers very often at first but not very seriously.' No wonder the reformers and workers were eager to set up a factory inspectorate; no wonder the employers resisted.

Workers in the fields were spared the dangers of machinery, but conditions were often just as intolerable. A father of an eleven-year-old girl told the 1843 Commission:

> I'm forced to let my daughter go, else I'm very much against it . . . they drive them along – force them along – they make them work hard. Gathering stones has hurt my girl's back at times. Pulling turnips is the hardest work; they get such a hold of the ground with their roots . . . It blisters their hands so that they can hardly touch anything. My girl went five miles to her work yesterday, turniping; she set off between seven and eight: she walked; had a piece of bread before she went; she did not stop work in the middle of the day; ate nothing till she left off . . . Their walks are worse than their work; she is sometimes so tired, she can't eat no victuals when she comes home.

Such heart-breaking evidence was all too common.

The government responded to these reports, and slowly

introduced new legislation. Employment in mines and textile factories, the worst black spots, was regulated by the Act of 1842, and protection was extended to children in many other trades in 1864.

How could such callousness have survived so long? The answer lies partly in the historical attitude towards children, whom many still considered to be not little cherubs in velvet jackets, but little adult imps full of sin, naturally evil, who needed to be kept out of mischief and beaten out of wickedness. The children's literature of the period shows some very harsh attitudes – for example, the immensely popular *History of the Fairchild Family*, by Mrs Sherwood, which went through countless editions during Victoria's reign. She believed that children were destined for hell unless severely punished and lectured every day; to instruct the little Fairchilds in morality, their father takes them to see a rotting corpse hanging from a gibbet. Clearly a generation that thought this a suitable afternoon outing for a middle-class child would not be too squeamish at the sight of a working-class child pulling turnips.

Then, again, there is the recurrent theme of infant mortality. It would be quite wrong to suggest that because the Victorians expected to lose some of their children, they therefore did not love them or grieve over their loss; the turnip puller's father was obviously deeply concerned for his child, and the novelist Mrs Gaskell, who lost her only son from scarlet fever when he was ten months old, never forgot him. Nevertheless, it is true that many children were expected to die, and were treated with a carelessness that often caused their deaths. Partly through ignorance, babies were given totally unsuitable drugs made from laudanum and opium, and were frequently dosed with gin. Illegitimate babies, and babies of working mothers, were 'farmed out' to women who let them die more or less on purpose, pocketing the farming money as they did so. It was not uncommon, late in the nineteenth century, to find dead babies in the streets of London. In this climate, it is not surprising that children were treated with severity, and expected to work if they were able. But as the century wore on, there was a gradual quickening of the social conscience; orphans and paupers were treated less as criminals, more as victims. As early as 1837, Dickens portrayed the miseries of the workhouse child in *Oliver Twist*; there were growing numbers of Ragged Schools and Shaftsbury Homes for the poor; in 1870 Dr Barnardo opened his first home for destitute boys. Schemes for training the homeless were established; other philanthropists arranged to transport them to a new, and, they hoped, better life in the colonies.

The child's lot was also vastly improved by a drop in family size, improved sanitation in cities, and a recognition, in the Education Acts of 1870 and 1876, of the right of all children to elementary education – and incidentally, to food. The school dinner was introduced in recognition of the fact that a child cannot work on an empty stomach, and although rarely popular in our more affluent day, it was a real blessing to underfed children at the end of the last century.

Even the tone of sermons on early death changed. The subject was still popular, but it began to lose the fire-and-brimstone passion of Mrs Sherwood. In the popular sermons of the Reverend James Vaughan, preached specially for children in Brighton in the 1860s, we find plenty of stories about poor children dying of hunger and sickness, but the tone is much more consoling and reassuring. Heaven is waiting for the good; 'God take care of the baby' are one baby's dying words, and a little girl from a Ragged School, who went into domestic service and 'fell out of a window she was cleaning, and got her back broken, and both her legs, and one of her arms' (!) is dispatched to heaven happily, with the words: 'Oh, I am made so much of: all are so kind to me: I am afraid I shall get proud: I had better die and go to heaven.' This is morbid, but not cruel.

One ought to note, also, that the Victorian age was the first to produce a large and cheerful literature written specifically for children, without any moral and puritanical overtones. Edward Lear's nonsense books, published between 1846 and 1870, and Lewis Carroll's Alice books, with their superbly imaginative illustrations by Tenniel, were written to entertain. The idea of frightening children for their own good had gone so much out

of fashion that Carroll and Tenniel agreed to remove the Jabberwock from the frontispiece of *Through the Looking Glass* (1872)
to a less conspicuous part of the book (see plate 34). A new spirit,
and a much more kindly one. It was this period that formed our
modern concept of childhood as a privileged time, when play,
however serious, is still play; Richard Jefferies, a farmer's son,
created a new kind of hero of children's literature in *Bevis:
The Story of a Boy*, published in 1882. *Bevis* shows a great love
of countryside activities, such as fishing, hunting, and swimming,
and it presents these activities coloured by the intense light of a
boy's imagination; it is a world of make-believe, but it is also
real and complete in itself. Mark and Bevis are real boys, left
to amuse themselves by friendly, helpful, but on the whole
absent adults. They are healthy and active and enterprising and
do not waste the summer by reflecting morbidly on death; such
messages as the author has, about co-operation, kindness, friend-
ship and respect for the natural world are well hidden in the
story, not preached as from a pulpit.

The attitude towards women also underwent vast changes
during this period. The history of the emancipation of women
shows in very clear contrast the two nations, the rich and the
poor – or, more accurately, the middle class and the working class.
Broadly, the working woman needed protection from long hours
of work, whereas the impoverished middle-class woman needed
the *right* to work. Working women were then employed, like
children, in jobs that we would now think wholly unsuitable –
down the mines, in brickyards, in the potteries where they suffered
from lead poisoning, in match factories where they suffered
from sulphur poisoning, in textile factories, where their long hair
and impractical dress caused horrible accidents. There is no space
to describe the range of their misery. No wonder the working-
class home was often a bare and comfortless place, when mothers
were forced, through necessity, to work long hours, and to
return to work too soon after childbirth. Indeed sometimes the
home itself was turned into a small factory, with a whole family
working long hours to scratch a living (see plate 35). Amazingly
some of these women managed to keep their spirits up; commiss-

34. Tenniel's Jabberwock.

35. Matchbox-makers at Bow, 1871.

ioners note that women working in the pot banks or brick works
'are always singing. If there is anything new in the way of a song,
they are bound to have it . . . they love a joke, the rougher and
ruder the better.' (1864.)

The notorious immorality of the working women shocked some
inquirers, who were grieved to note that 'St Helens is not a very
moral place; there are dancing saloons all over town . . .' One
employer was shocked that other people were shocked when he
discharged a single woman simply because she was pregnant;
he thought he was behaving in a thoroughly proper way. There
were some women independent enough to prefer factory life to
the more secure life of domestic service – though domestic
service was much the most popular female occupation. In 1851,
there were 905,000 female domestics.

Gradually, the conscience of the age became uneasy about
the gulf between ideal womanhood and the labouring woman.
The seamstress became a particular focus of guilt, partly because

of the all-too-striking contrast between the elegant sewing which amused the housewife, and the appallingly paid, eye-ruining labour of the worker (see plate 36). Such women, whether they worked at home or for an employer, could hardly earn enough to

36. Two views of the plight of the seamstress: one compassionate, one savage. (See also page 86.)

(a) *The Song of the Shirt*, a painting by G. F. Watts.

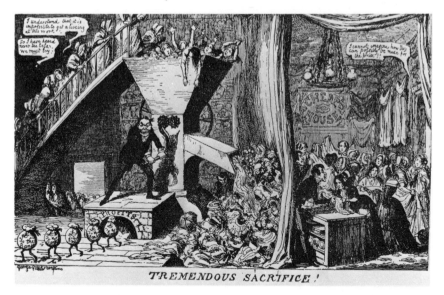

(b) *Tremendous Sacrifice*, a cartoon by George Cruickshank.
(See also page 85.)

keep alive, and Thomas Hood's poem, *The Song of the Shirt*,
published anonymously in *Punch* in 1843, put into words the
misery endured by thousands:

> Oh! men with sisters dear,
> Oh! men with mothers and wives,
> It is not linen you're wearing out,
> But human creatures' lives.

This poem became a popular theme for illustration, and was
treated by John Leech in *Punch* (1843), Richard Redgrave
(1844) and G. F. Watts (1850).

Educated women also suffered at this period. The paintings of
Richard Redgrave are fine illustrations of their barren, hard-
working lives. *The Poor Teacher* stresses the predicament of the
poor genteel girl who had to work for her living, who was
prevented by law and tradition and lack of higher training from
entering the more profitable professions. It was late in the century,
after much agitation, that legislation opened the door to medicine,
the law, the universities, the civil service. Before that, all a

respectable woman could do was to teach – or, of course, to write. This is why so many of the novels of the period have governesses as their heroines; it was a much feared fate. Jane Austen's Emma Watson says 'I would rather be a teacher at a school (and I can think of nothing worse) than marry a man I did not like', to which her sister replies, 'I would rather do anything than be a teacher at a school.' But some had no choice. The most notable examples are the Brontë sisters, for whose lives *The Poor Teacher* could be an illustration. Emily, the most independent, hated teaching so much that she abandoned it, but Charlotte and Anne, almost as miserable, stuck it out for years, leaving their bitter testimony in *Jane Eyre, Villette,* and *Agnes Gray.* The Brontës and Redgrave catch the desolate solitude of such women, cut off from their family, alone in a strange world, neither servant nor gentlewoman, condemned to lead a meek life of thankless service. The woman in the painting is reading a black-bordered letter, announcing the death of a loved one; the words of the song on the piano read 'Home, sweet home'. (Redgrave's own sister Jane worked as a governess, and returned home to die young of typhoid fever, a sadly familiar story in real life as well as in novels.) In the original painting, there were no children playing in the background; Redgrave added them at the purchaser's request. Without them, he said, the painting was too sad (see plate 37).

Such protests gradually had effect. Schools and colleges for women were founded; among the earliest were Queen's College, Harley Street, and the Ladies' College, Cheltenham. The working hours of working women were restricted by factory acts. Some recognized that the position of women needed the most radical change; John Stuart Mill, when he married his wife Harriet in 1851, signed a document renouncing the rights which the law conferred on him over her 'person, property and freedom of action', a gesture which was followed in 1880 by the Married Women's Property Act, which allowed women to keep their own property and money after marriage, instead of handing it over to their husbands. It is hard to imagine that Mrs Gaskell had to hand over her own literary earnings to her husband, as she was

37. Richard Redgrave's painting *The Poor Teacher*.

not legally entitled to them or to a bank account of her own, and when she wanted to buy a new country house to surprise him, she had to do it behind his back, with the help of a son-in-law. Mill's essay, *The Subjection of Women* (1869) was an important landmark. But the demand for the vote (which made the Queen 'so furious she can not contain herself', according to one witness) was not fulfilled until 1918, and in the 1970s we have found it necessary to introduce an Equal Pay Act and an Equal Opportunities Commission.

The working conditions of the poor were shocking. Their living conditions were no better. The Dickensian London of cellars and alleyways and snuggeries and rotting warehouses, the Manchester of Engels and Mrs Gaskell, where children died of hunger and cholera in dank, overcrowded basements, were places of misery and horror. The problems were caused by the population increase and the drift to the cities, and it took decades of effort to solve them – or even to make some admit that they needed solving. The idea of sanitation as a public responsibility was new, and many took the view (familiar to us from those who defend the right to die by nicotine poisoning) that the government had no right to meddle in such matters. *The Times*, which disliked the reforming zeal of sewage enthusiast Chadwick, declared in 1858, when London's first modern sewer was planned: 'We prefer to take our chance with cholera and the rest than be bullied into health. England wants to be clean, but not be cleaned by Chadwick.'

Housing, too, was a free-for-all, hotchpotch affair; town planning did not exist. Mine owners, recognizing that miners needed houses, built the depressing terraces that stride across the hilltops of the north of England (see plate 38), but in the big cities the ever-growing numbers of the poor had to force their way into cellars and crowd families into one room. Peter Conrad, in a fine picture of Victorian England called *The Victorian Treasure House*, points out that the poor were 'subterraneous, inhabiting a literal underworld'; London had become 'a warren of caves and hiding places, secretly connected', over which hung the smog which Dickens evokes so brilliantly in the first paragraphs of *Bleak House*:

38. Victorian housing still standing in twentieth-century Newcastle-upon-Tyne.

Smoke, lowering down from chimney-pots, making a soft black drizzle, with flakes of soot in it as big as snow flakes – gone into mourning, one might imagine, for the death of the sun.

Less poetically, the reformer Dr Simon claimed that smoke made London 'the unsightliest metropolis in Europe'. This was the price we paid for being ahead in the industrial race. Committees investigated housing, health, smoke abatement, set up a Public Health Act in 1852, an Act for Improving Artisans' Dwellings in 1875, working gradually towards our present attitudes.

We have many pictures of city life at this period. There were colourful and picturesque elements, as well as squalid. Dickens obviously had a great affection for the ramshackle disorder of London, with its thieves' dens and cobbled courtyards, in which people could make cosy little hiding holes and build their own little fantasies, without any nonsense about planning permission. Mr Wemmick's house at Walworth, in *Great Expectations*, is a perfect example of free enterprise; out of the tiniest wooden cottage, he has made a fortified castle, with gothic windows, a flagstaff, a moat four feet wide and two feet deep, an ornamental lake, and a gun protected from the rain by 'an ingenious little tarpaulin contrivance in the nature of an umbrella'. (Note, too, the division of work and home life – Wemmick, at home, is an affectionate son to his Aged Parent, and a warm-hearted host, but at work he is a hard-faced man of business.) Gustave Doré, who did many engravings of London, also revealed the clutter and confusion as picturesque, conscious though he was of the extreme poverty they represented (see plate 39).

Even Mayhew, whose famous study of *London Labour and the London Poor* reveals some horrifying statistics, has an eye for the beautiful in the midst of squalor; after a vivid description of Jacob's Island in London's dockland of Bermondsey, the pestilential capital of cholera and 'Venice of drains', washed by reeking sewage the colour of strong green tea, he dwells with relief on the sight of a single red dahlia in a garden:

39. Gustave Dore's *Over London by Rail*.

Never was colour so grateful to the eye. All we had looked at had been so dark and dingy, and had smelt so much of churchyard clay, that this little patch of beauty was brighter even than an oasis in the desert. (London Characters, 1874.)

But in their hearts most people knew that, as Dickens wrote during a visit to Edinburgh, picturesqueness and typhus were 'fast friends'. Much as we regret the winding, cobbled streets of the past, they were rightly recognized as breeding grounds for disease (see plate 40). Long before cholera was understood, the physician John Snow established that the outbreak of 1854 could be traced to one source – the contaminated Broad Street pump in Golden Square. Chadwick, Snow and Simon waged a prolonged battle against overcrowding, bad drains and overflowing grave-

40. *A Court for King Cholera*, a cartoon of 1852 drawing attention to the
conditions, ignored by many, which bred disease.

yards. Their efforts may not have appeared as romantic as
Florence Nightingale's but they were as important. Simon
complained that the waterworks of the Romans were better than
those of Victorian London, and disputed the widely held belief
that the poor did not *want* to be cleaned up; most people think,
he says, that 'if you give them a coal scuttle, a washing basin or a
water closet, these several utensils will be applied indifferently
to the purposes of each other . . .' (City Medical Reports, 1849.)
It sounds like the old story, of miners who keep coals in the bath.
    In 1854, George Godwin, editor of *The Builder*, published a
book called *London Shadows; A Glance at the 'Homes' of
Thousands*, which gives a shocking account of housing conditions.
He describes 'places not fit for dogs, yet which hold in every
room two or three families'. A typical dwelling is that of a
woodchopper off Gray's Inn Road. The whole family lives in one

(a) A stranger clean from the country. An inhabitant of Hyde Park.

(b) The Dead and the Living: Bishopsgate-street district.

41. Two drawings from George Godwin's *London Shadows*.

room, with no bedsteads, chairs or tables, but a few heaps of ragged clothes. The engravings show unplanned, higgledy-piggledy developments, the great black smoke clouds of industry, the effects of pollution (see plate 41a). But the aspect of over-crowding that worried Godwin and his colleagues most was that the dead had to share space with the living, sometimes for many days (see plate 41b). There are many macabre tales on this theme, but the worst is Godwin's, who recounts that on

> Opening a cupboard in a miserable room in Gray's Inn Lane, we found, shut up with the bread and some other matters, *the body of a child*, without a coffin, but decently disposed. The child had been dead a week: on one of the shelves was its little mug, marked Mary Ann.

This is not sentimentality, like the saintly death of little Nell – it is realism.

The novelists, as well as the sanitary reformers, played their part in arousing the awareness of the more fortunate. During the 1840s, novels about the poor began to replace novels about the rich. In 1838, Carlyle attacked the kind of book that described only polite society, and Disraeli, Dickens and Mrs Gaskell were among the leaders of the new novelists writing of working-class life. *Fraser's Magazine* recommended Mrs Gaskell's *Mary Barton* because it would explain to the well-fed with their Turkey carpets why 'brave, honest, industrious north-country hearts' were maddened by poverty into strikes and violence.

By the end of the century, writers like George Bernard Shaw and H. G. Wells could address themselves directly to working men. Electoral reform, education acts, and the trade unions had given the workers the power to fight for their own rights. The great gulf between the two nations was no longer accepted with complacency, as the will of God. Many hoped that a bright new age of social equality was about to dawn.

THE ARTS

ARCHITECTURE AND PAINTING

As we saw in the account of the Great Exhibition, the great age of scientific progress also produced a rebellion against industry and the machine. While business boomed, poets, painters and architects retreated from the ugliness of the modern world into a nostalgic attempt to recreate the past. One of the earliest and most influential spirits of this new movement was the architect and designer, Pugin (1812–1852), who was an ardent believer in the revival of the gothic style. He looked back to the Middle Ages as a time of spiritual and artistic harmony. The Reformation and the architecture of the Renaissance had, in his view, combined to destroy the spirit of craftsmanship and dedication in which the great cathedrals and churches had been built. He saw modern building as a confused and ugly jumble of styles, inappropriately applied, and complained: 'We have Swiss cottages in a flat country; Italian villas in the coldest situations; a Turkish Kremlin for a royal residence'; (i.e., Brighton Pavilion) 'Greek temples in crowded lanes.' He thought the classical, Palladian style which dominated the eighteenth century was debased, heartless, and pagan; in contrast, the gothic was Christian and romantic.

To him, architecture was more than a trade, more even than a craft; it was a religious expression. Like many of his contemporaries, he was searching for a new Christian commitment, as a protest against the uglier aspects of Protestant greed and materialism, and he found it in the Roman Catholic Church, which he joined in 1834. This was the time of the flourishing Oxford Movement, lead by Cardinal Newman, and Pugin was one of many distinguished converts to the Catholic faith. His ideas had a far-reaching influence, and transformed the appearance of our cities, which are full of churches and public buildings designed in the gothic style; his followers inherited his spiritual passion, and architecture became a subject of intense religious debate and controversy. Many gothic designers had, like Pugin, a missionary zeal. His greatest monument is one of the most familiar buildings in Britain: the Houses of Parliament, on which he collaborated with Sir Charles Barry, are a tribute to his short life of intense and enthusiastic labour. Both the general style, and the stress on detail and craftsmanship of carving, are characteristic. The building has had many critics, but, as Lord Clark aptly says in one of the first twentieth-century reappraisals of nineteenth-century gothic, 'We cannot rid our imagination of that extraordinary building which seems to embody all that is most characteristic and most moving in London.' Most Londoners and most tourists would agree.

Not all his works are as successful. Some of his designs appear to our taste over-elaborate, over-decorated, and inappropriate – why should a country house look like a medieval chapel, and who would want dining room chairs that looked like the furnishings of a baronial hall, or a dining table like a church altar? Pugin thought his fellow designers were faithless pagans; we find some of his work excessively religious. He had something of the fanatic, in him, and was a splendid advocate of his own ideas. His book, *Contrasts*, first published in 1836 and reprinted in a slightly more moderate form in 1841, is an impassioned and persuasive attack on modern ugliness. He was a fine draughtsman, and his contrasts between the old and the new are left largely to speak for themselves in illustrations – he shows us, for example, an imaginary city landscape from 1440, full – perhaps overfull – of pointing spires and crosses, side by side with a city view of 1840, disfigured by bleak warehouses, sewage works and factory chimneys, a city completely subdued to industry and necessity.

6. *Belshazzar's Feast* by John Martin.

7. *Astarte Syriaca:* Dante Gabriel Rossetti's
painting of Jane Morris.

(Gothic architecture was sometimes known as pointed architecture: one can find peculiarly uncomfortable pointed gothic chairs.) Similarly, Pugin contrasts the dignity and modesty of figures on a medieval altar with the 'loose and indecent costume and postures of the figures intended for saints' on an eighteenth-century one: the latter are, he says, more suited to a fashionable boudoir. Most telling of all, perhaps, is his beautiful drawing of Chichester Cross, which he contrasts with a ridiculous monument to George IV, with a police station stuck in its base (see plate 42).

Pugin died young, but his influence lived, fostered by his disciples. Sir Gilbert Scott, William Butterfield and Philip Webb preached the gothic revival in theory and practice; Scott's Albert Memorial (see plate 43) and Butterfield's church in Margaret Street are two widely differing but characteristic achievements of the movement. One of Pugin's warmest admirers was John Ruskin (1819–1900), who shared many of his prejudices. Ruskin was a powerful ally, for his writings were immensely popular, and his opinions could make or break an artist's career.

King's Cross Battle Bridge,   Chichester Cross.
a monument to George IV.

42. One of Pugin's contrasts.

43. The Albert Memorial.

He gave his blessing to the Pre-Raphaelite Brotherhood, a group of artists who, like Pugin, sought inspiration from a medieval past. Like him, they had a sense of religious dedication to art, though the private lives of some of them were far from spiritual; Millais, one of the founder members, was to marry Ruskin's wife Effie, after a celebrated scandal. Other founder members were Dante Gabriel Rossetti, poet and painter, and Holman Hunt, whose *Light of the World* is as well known as Millais's *Bubbles*. The PRB had a curious reputation; despite their high-mindedness, many of their works were thought to be 'nasty', perhaps because of the sensuousness of their style, and the beauty of their models. They created a taste for a certain style of female beauty, still described as Pre-Raphaelite; the most striking living examples were Janey Morris, wife of William Morris, whose sultry, passionate heavy face gazes at us from many of Rossetti's paintings, and Elizabeth Siddal, Rossetti's wife, who was the group's favourite model for years, and who is famed for having lain patiently for many hours in a tepid bath while posing for Millais's dying *Ophelia*. With their long, rippling flowing hair and their full mouths, they are real 'stunners' – (the curiously un-Victorian PRB word for a beauty) – and their many portraits are a defiant protest against the myth of the sexless, tidy Victorian miss (see colour plate 7).

The beliefs of the PRB are hard to categorize. Truth to nature was one – hence the realistic posing in the bath, and the careful botanical detail of the flowers amidst which Ophelia drowns. Paintings should be fresh and bright – trees were green in nature, although brown in the works of the Old Masters, so the PRB followed nature rather than tradition, and painted trees green. Hence the rather shocking brightness of some of their work. The old Masters, like Sir Joshua (Sloshua) Reynolds, sloshed the paint on: the PRB painted with precision. Truth was considered to be more important than beauty, an opinion which produced Millais's *Christ in the House of his Parents*, of which Dickens wrote indignantly that Christ appears as 'a hideous, wrynecked, blubbering red-haired boy in a nightgown', and the Virgin Mary as 'so horrible in her ugliness that . . . she would stand out from the rest of the company as a monster in the vilest cabaret in France or in the lowest ginshop in England'. Symbolism was much used; Holman Hunt's *Scapegoat* (to paint which he travelled all the way to the Dead Sea) is a classic example, though many seemingly narrative paintings, such as his *The Awakening Conscience* or Rossetti's *Found* are also full of symbolism. They were particularly fond of romantic historical subjects from Shakespeare, Keats and Tennyson, and from Arthurian legend. Some of them tackled the ugliness of the modern world, and handled contemporary themes, but the main emphasis was on the past, which makes their work now look curiously escapist for a movement that saw itself as rebellious, avant-garde, anti-traditional. Burne-Jones, a late disciple, who

loved to paint nymphs and knights, Greek gods and angels,
declared that the more materialistic science became, the more
angels he would paint – a despairing cry of a lost cause, rather
than a challenge to the future.

The PRB did not have a monopoly of symbolism. The successful painter George Frederic Watts, close friend of Tennyson,
liked allegorical subjects such as *Time and Oblivion, Love and
Life, Satan and Sin*. Perhaps his most famous painting is that
peculiarly Victorian work, *Hope*, which shows a blind woman
sitting on top of the world with a lyre – though it is an interesting
comment on Victorian taste and prudery to find that a reproduc-
tion of this figure, still so popular in hotels and boarding houses,
was once rejected for a seaman's chapel on grounds of impro-
priety. Less overtly allegorical is his portrait of his wife, the
actress Ellen Terry; it is called *Choosing*, and in it we see her
attempt to choose between the large but scentless camelia, and
the bunch of modest but fragrant violets which she clutches to
her heart (see plate 44).

The Victorians, as will by now be obvious, loved paintings
that told a story; they read them as we read books. Titles like
The Last Day in the Old Home, The Empty Purse, and *Home
from the Sea* were attached to paintings packed with clues for the
careful observer to decipher. Augustus Egg's *Past and Present
(No 1)* has enough material for a whole novel; in it we see the
despairing husband clutching an incriminating letter, while
his guilty wife lies on the carpet by a symbolically worm-eaten
apple; behind her the two children whose family life is in ruins
look up from a symbolically tumbling house of cards (see plate
45). *The Poor Teacher* and *Woman's Mission*, reproduced earlier,
are equally full of information. It is always worth trying to 'read'
even the patterns on the wallpaper in paintings of this kind;
every detail (and the artists loved detail) may tell a story. Millais
was described in a memorial tribute as a 'novelist . . . a great
story teller'.

Huge crowd scenes, celebrating buoyant Victorian life, were
also popular. The master of this genre was W. P. Frith, who
chose subjects like *Ramsgate Sands* (1854), *Derby Day* (1858)

44. *Choosing*: G. F. Watts's portrait of his wife, Ellen Terry.

(see colour plate 8) and *The Railway Station* (1862), and who filled every corner with people and incidents, just as the housewife filled every corner of her house. Far from avoiding contemporary

45. Augustus Egg's painting *Past and Present (No. 1)*.

life, he enjoys it. William Bell Scott said of him: 'Frith will be much thought of in some future day, because he illustrated the age in which we live . . .' – yet, interestingly, goes on to add that Victorian paintings will be less valued as documentary records than earlier ones, such as Hogarth's, because 'our pictorial newspapers now narrow the field for the painter in this respect'. This view reflects the fear that photography, a relatively new invention, would permanently diminish the importance and function of art; why imitate what the camera could do better? Some thought art and the new science could be reconciled, and used photographs to aid their memories; David Octavius Hill, who became an outstanding portrait photographer, once painted a group with 474 individual likenesses, and understandably found photographs an invaluable aid. Frith denied that he had 'cheated' in this way – ('Every object, living or dead, was painted from nature,' he said of his *Paddington Station*) – but many think he used photographic help for *Derby Day*, and he admitted later to using it to portray royalty. Frith and Scott were right to suspect a threat; Frith's kind of work was indeed to go permanently out of fashion, and although we now admire his huge crowds, we note a certain frozen lifelessness in all the bustle. It was left to the Impressionists to paint movement; they too enjoyed crowd scenes, but their approach was to be entirely different, less detailed, less documentary.

If artists used photography, photographers imitated art. Composite group portraits were fabricated from different negatives. Roger Fenton's wonderful photographs of the Crimean War, while bringing the immediacy of warfare home to those in Britain, are nevertheless carefully posed – as they had to be, with the long exposures then necessary. Perhaps the most famous of Victorian photographers was Julia Margaret Cameron, close friend of many of the great men of her day, including Tennyson; she took many traditional photographic portraits of her contemporaries, but also delighted in dressing her subjects as King Arthur, John the Baptist, or a Greek muse (see plate 46). Many of her works are more Pre-Raphaelite than the Pre-Raphaelites, and her sitters, like Elizabeth Siddal, had to endure agonies of discomfort; one niece recalls:

> Our roles were no less than those of the Two Angels of the Nativity, and to sustain them we were scantily clad and each had a pair of heavy swan wings fastened to her narrow shoulders, while Aunt Julia, with ungentle hand, touzled our hair to get rid of the prim nursery look. No wonder those old photographs of us, leaning over imaginary ramparts of heaven, look anxious and wistful . . .(Lady Troubridge).

One of the few painters to look beyond the realistic conventions of the time, and to foreshadow the development of Impressionism and even the concept of abstract art, was American-born James McNeill Whistler (1834–1903). His outlook was much broader than that of his English contemporaries, for he was

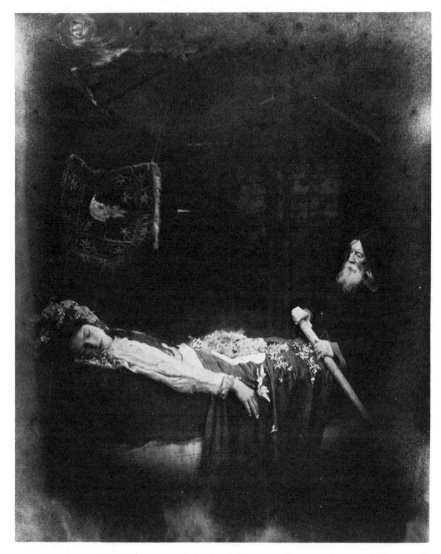

46. *Lancelot and Elaine*, one of Julia Margaret Cameron's carefully posed photographs.

widely travelled and familiar with French art in particular, but his work of the 1860s clearly shows his close association with the Pre-Raphaelites, and a fashionable preoccupation with Chinese and Japanese art. But his work became increasingly original;

47. Whistler's *Harmony in Grey and Green*,
a portrait of Miss Cicely Alexander.

he took to giving his paintings abstract titles, calling them
'Symphonies', 'Nocturnes' and 'Arrangements', stressing his
departure from realism (see plate 47). He moved too far and too
fast for some of his contemporaries; in 1877 Ruskin attacked his

Falling Rocket in violent terms, saying it was 'flinging a pot of paint in the public's face', and Whistler was forced into a libel action to defend his good name; he won it, but was awarded only a farthing's damages. The court case left him bankrupt and, in the eyes of the public, ridiculous; then as now, the majority were delighted to pour scorn on any artistic innovation they did not understand, and their Philistinism was encouraged by Ruskin's powerful support. Whistler fought back, and regained popularity and lasting acceptance; today, he stands out as one of the most creative and far-sighted artists of his day, whose broader vision stirred the complacency of British insularity.

A final word on Victorian art must go to Victoria's favourite artist, Landseer, if only because his work demonstrates such characteristic English qualities – a love of dogs and royalty, sentimentality about dying animals, a pleasure in hunting. The stags, dead and living, which adorn his canvasses are the essence of the spirit of Balmoral Castle, while his lions which guard Nelson's Column in Trafalgar Square have on their faces the smug expression of the British Empire as it liked to see itself. He was an artist in tune with the spirit of the age.

William Morris, on the other hand, though much more influential, was not at all in tune with his time. Like Ruskin and Pugin, he was ahead of it in some ways, yet in other ways wished to turn back the clock. A visionary socialist, he dreamed of a new world which would revive the crafts of the old. He was a talented painter, but, more significantly, he also had a passion for making things with his own hands. He learned to carve stone and wood, and discovered that his mission and social duty was to become a designer craftsman, and to train others to follow him and work in his workshops. His genius can be seen in every field of design – pottery, glass, metalwork, furniture, printing, fabrics, wallpaper.

One of the best ways to appreciate the impact of his work is to take a walk through the gallery of nineteenth-century furniture in the Victoria and Albert Museum. After a medley of mosaic and inlay and mother-of-pearl and papier-mâché, after enormous épergnes and Minton salt cellars with dolphins and shells, one walks suddenly into the shockingly, refreshingly familiar. The Morris designs are amazingly welcome to the eye, after the restlessness of those before. Yet they are by no means plain – his fabrics and papers, with names like Lily, Acanthus, Daisy, Pomegranate and Honeysuckle, are intricate, rich, satisfying (see plate 48). The patterns and shapes are observed from nature, but not obtrusively realistic; the colours are natural rather than synthetic and harsh. The patterns are still popular today – though unfortunately, and significantly, the handprinting processes they require make them very expensive, and price them out of the range of the average buyer, for whose taste and environment Morris had such concern.

48. 'Chrysanthemum' wallpaper design by William Morris.

Morris has been much criticized, for failing to come to terms with his times, for living in an unreal medieval past of guilds and arts-and-crafts, for imitating ancient models rather than creating new ones. (The architects of Pugin's gothic revival patronized his firm, Morris, Marshall Faulkner and Co, which learned to specialize in stained-glass windows – hardly the most useful of commodities for a committed socialist to produce.) He has been accused of making expensive articles for a wealthy middle class, while claiming to believe in Art for the People, like Ruskin. The art historian Timothy Hilton calls him 'a bloodless Utopian'. He himself admitted that he had to compromise his principles by designing for the rich, simply to ensure his firm's survival and when asked one day why he was looking so depressed, broke out with: 'It is only that I spend my life in ministering to the swinish luxury of the rich!' Yet the fact remains that the objects he made and inspired continue to delight the eye, and to affect our taste; so do those of his pupils and friends. The pottery of De Morgan, the furniture and architecture of E. W. Godwin, the cutlery of the arch-medievalist William Burges, the brass lampshades and firescreens of W. A. S. Benson are all objects that belong as much to our present as to a nineteenth-century or medieval past (see plate 49). Not only our museums, but also our homes are full of the results of his inspiration. He changed the appearance of Britain, by training his craftsmen to make, and succeeding generations to look and to care. He refused to believe that ordinary people were satisfied with cheap rubbish, and despised the cynical manufacturers' view that the public gets what it deserves. He swept away the clutter of half a century, by telling us that we should have nothing in our homes that we do not know to be useful or believe to be beautiful. In an age when most educated people considered working men incapable of appreciating art or culture, he insisted on the natural right of every man to live in beautiful surroundings. From him we inherit not only wallpaper, but a faith in democratic culture.

Nor were he and his followers adamantly opposed to the machine. Morris's carpets were machine woven, and Benson's copper work, strikingly original and beautiful, was designed

49. A brass and copper lamp by Benson, about 1895.

specifically for the new techniques. The debate over Handicrafts versus Machinery continues to rage, even today; Morris's men were, on the whole, in the former camp, but they responded to the challenge of the Great Exhibition with imagination and daring.

MUSIC

Most people, when asked to think of Victorian composers and Victorian music, look blank, and have to think hard before remembering any significant names. It was not an age of major achievement, though it produced some important developments, notably that of tonic sol-fa, and some lasting monuments in such British institutions as Hymns Ancient and Modern and Gilbert and Sullivan. But on the whole it was an age of do-it-yourself, of songs around the piano, of duets and choral societies and musical evenings. Before the invention of radio and the gramophone, home singing was much more popular than it is now, at all social levels. As so often, Prince Albert set the tone. He loved to play the organ and to sing; indeed, his enemies labelled him 'the operatic tenor'. He wrote music of his own, including the chorale 'In Life's Gay Morn', which Jenny Lind sang at the marriage of Edward VII. He was a close friend of Mendelssohn, whose organ accompaniments he played while the Queen sang. He supervised the Queen's private orchestra, encouraging her to hear works by Bach, Mozart, Schubert and Wagner, as well as the ever-respectable Handel and Haydn. Not all his subjects had the same opportunities for expressing their musical appreciation, but they followed his lead enthusiastically. George Henry Lewes, husband of the novelist George Eliot, loved to sing *O ruddier than the cherry* from Handel's *Acis and Galatea,* and at Moray Lodge, the home of Arthur Lewis, owner of a millinery firm in Regent Street, the Moray Minstrels who performed there, included the novelists Trollope and Thackeray, and artists Millais and Lord Leighton. A professional touch was added to musical evenings at Scott Russell's home in Norwood, near the transplanted Crystal Palace, where famous performers such as Patti would mingle with composers like Arthur Sullivan and music lovers like George Grove, Director of the Royal College of Music, still remembered for his *Grove's Dictionary of Music and Musicians.*

The invention of tonic sol-fa, a system of sight-singing still widely used, opened the pleasures of song to a whole new uneducated public. Its principal originator was a congregational minister, John Curwen, and it was disliked by some on much the same grounds that teaching the poor to read and write was disapproved – it would debase musical taste, and give the poor ideas above their station in life. Also, it smacked of hymn-singing Evangelism, still not wholly respectable to Church-of-England Victorians. But it was too useful a method to be sneered out of existence, and by its help, working men could become choralists and form working-men's choirs. The seal of respectability was set on hymn-singing when *Hymns Ancient and Modern* appeared in 1861, a volume that sold one hundred million copies in its first ninety years of life, and which united in one volume the songs of the Methodist John Wesley and Cardinal Newman of the Oxford Movement, and music by Bach, Purcell, Parry, Stanford, and the tireless Reverend John Bacchus Dykes, whose works include those favourites 'Nearer my God to thee', 'Jesus lover of my soul', and Newman's 'Lead kindly light', as well as many others.

The names of three composers of serious music stand out from the general musical apathy and ignorance. The earliest was Sterndale Bennett, admirer and friend of Mendelssohn. Mendelssohn's influence in Britain was considerable; he visited the country many times, composed *Fingal's Cave* after a tour of the Hebrides, and conducted the first performance of *Elijah* at Birmingham in 1846. His works remained popular long after his death in 1847. But Sterndale Bennett had difficulties in achieving proper recognition, and spent most of his life teaching. In the last quarter of the century, as musical education and appreciation spread, aided by such institutions as the Royal College of Music, the Cambridge University Musical Society and Manchester's Hallé Orchestra, there was a marked revival of British music, led by Sir Charles Stanford and Sir Hubert Parry. Stanford (1852–1924), organist and composer, set a new standard for church music, composed symphonies (several of which were performed at the Crystal Palace), oratorios, songs and part songs, and was also a brilliant teacher of composition, influencing a generation of pupils during his many years at the Royal College. Parry

(1848–1918), who studied under Sterndale Bennett, produced some magnificent choral works, such as 'Blest Pair of Sirens', first performed by the Bach choir in 1887, and his setting of Blake's *Jerusalem* is of course still widely sung throughout the country. In 1894 he succeeded George Grove as the Director of the Royal College of Music. Apart from music, his great passion was athletics, in which he indulged, apparently, with a fine recklessness, careless of life or limb – a typical all-round English gentleman, of the classic Eton–Oxford variety.

Typically English, too, in a different way, is the work of the couple who achieved the most resounding success of all in the world of Victorian music, Gilbert and Sullivan. We always think of them together, though in fact Arthur Sullivan had an independent and separate career as a serious composer of sacred music, symphonies, and best-selling sentimental songs such as 'The Lost Chord', which the Prince of Wales declared he would travel the length of his kingdom to hear. He also preceded Stanford as director of Leeds Festival, where his oratorio *The Golden Legend* was hailed in 1886 as a work of genius, and Sullivan himself as the Mozart of Britain. Gilbert, for his part, was successful before their collaboration as the author of the satirical *Bab Ballads*. But their lasting fame rests on their light operas, such as *H.M.S. Pinafore, Patience* and *Iolanthe*, which are perhaps too well known to every school dramatic society and every amateur operatic group to need description (see plate 50). Their partnership was far from harmonious in personal terms, but in their work they achieved a balance of wit, pathos, popular common sense and mild satire that proved a perfect recipe for late-Victorian audiences. They both mock and celebrate the English way of life, with splendid flights of verbal and musical fancy. Light opera had hitherto been dominated by French composers such as Offenbach, whose pieces did not adapt very satisfactorily to the more prudish English stage; Gilbert and Sullivan provided a home-grown variety, topical and sparkling, yet decent enough for the Queen herself – who, while encouraging dear Sir Arthur to write a serious opera, preferred to command performances of *The Gondoliers* at Windsor. There is something immensely

8. *Derby Day* by W. P. Frith.

9. One of Marianne North's many paintings
of flora in Western Australia.

50. Music cover for Chappell's edition of *Iolanthe*.

safe, no-nonsense, and slightly Philistine about Gilbert and Sullivan; nowadays we may prickle at slighting references to lady novelists 'who never would be missed', at the patronizing quaintness of the Japan of the *Mikado*, at the mockery of the 'greenery-yallery, Grosvenor Gallery, foot-in-the-grave young

man' of *Patience*, all of which show the kind of instinctive
Philistinism and insularity which Matthew Arnold condemned
in the British middle classes. They are, like Victoria herself,
essentially middle class, and therefore all the more representative
of their age. But they have lasted well beyond that age, and are
still as much loved as ever – whether that is a tribute to the
unchanging nature of British taste, or to the timeless wit and
charm of their inventions, is a doubtful point.

The working classes had their music too. The hymn singing
of the Evangelical movement was a genuinely popular pastime,
and, on a less lofty level, the public houses were full of songs and
entertainments. Most taverns had music rooms; the Coal Hole in
the Strand and Evans's Song-and-Supper Rooms in Covent
Garden were well known for their late-night programmes of
comedy and singing. Cheap song books of words, and less often
of music, were widely sold in penny numbers; the songs had such
titles as 'Darling Nelly Gray', 'Willie on the Dark Blue Sea', and
'Beautiful Star'. A modern scholar investigating the songs of
miners in the nineteenth century found a living oral tradition,
but also discovered the words of ballads in broadsides, pocket
songsters, local newspapers, and the files of the United Mine
Workers Journal. American songs were imported, in collections
like *Uncle Tom's Song Book*, exploiting the success of *Uncle
Tom's Cabin*. The composer Berlioz, on a visit to the Great
Exhibition, heard black-faced minstrel troupes in London
singing American ballads. While there was little serious theatre,
there was a great deal of commercial entertainment: one gets a
good idea of the kind of show staged from reading that Gilbert's
play for the Lyceum pantomime in 1867 was interrupted, to his
annoyance, by tableaux like a Fairy Aquarium with Espinosa's
Grand Ballet, St James's Park After a Snowstorm, and the
Electric Light and Magic Fountain.

The Edwardian age was the great age of music-hall, which
blossomed under the patronage of Edward VII, but there were
well-known singers working throughout the Victorian period;
Jenny Hill, a cabdriver's daughter, billed as the 'Vital Spark',
made a fortune and bought a large house in Streatham before

51. Cover for the sheet music of *Oh! Mr Porter*, one of Marie Lloyd's most popular songs.

she died in 1896, and Marie Lloyd, who first appeared in 1885, made famous such songs as 'My Old Man said Follow the Van' and 'Oh! Mr Porter' (see plate 51). The nineteenth century in

England may be lacking in great composers, but it was not lacking in musical activity on many levels; most importantly, perhaps, as it taught the illiterate to read, so it taught an ignorant public to listen and to sing, spreading appreciation of music throughout the provinces, and throughout the social scale, preparing the nation for the widespread availability of good music on record and radio, as well as at concerts and theatres.

POETRY

Victorian poetry, like Victorian art, tends to be nostalgic and escapist. It imitates old forms, and dwells on historical subjects; it prefers flowers and trees to city life. It creates a dream world, and its rhythms lull the reader to sleep. Take, at random, lines from Tennyson:

> The woods decay, the woods decay and fall,
> The vapours weep their burthen to the ground,
> Man comes and tills the field and lies beneath,
> And after many a summer dies the swan.

or 'Mariana at the Moated Grange', a favourite subject of illustrators (see plate 52), whose refrain is

> I am aweary, aweary,
> I would that I were dead.

This is the island of the lotos-eaters; poetry is a world of languor and vague melancholy. There are of course exceptions, in the disconcerting metres of Browning, the experiments of Gerard Manley Hopkins, the satirical verse of Clough, who was fond of such irreverent jingles as

> There is no God, the wicked saith,
> And truly it's a blessing,
> For what he might have done with us
> It's better only guessing.

There are exceptions, too, in subject matter; Tennyson attempted to write of modern ideas and inventions, tackling the new Darwinian concept of nature, not benevolent, but red in tooth

52. Millais's painting of Tennyson's *Mariana at the Moated Grange.*

and claw, and drawing poetic images from the railways. But the dominant tone, unlike that of the more political earlier romantics, remains one of weariness. The fondness for historical subjects betrays a certain lack of creative energy, a feeling that poetry was not really capable of dealing with the confusion of modern life. Victorian verse was responsible for the view, still widely held, that poetry properly deals with specifically poetic and elevated themes, rather than with immediate reality. Earlier poets such as Shelley and Wordsworth had no such opinions, but Victorian poets, with a lofty earnestness, looked to the past for inspiration, closing their eyes to the smoke and squalor around them.

Tennyson's favourite period was the age of chivalry and courtly romance (see plate 53). Sir Galahad and King Arthur, Launcelot and Guinevere, provided him, as well as the Pre-Raphaelites, with inspiration. Like many of his contemporaries, he imitated the medieval ballad form, but one of his best-loved works was a blank verse epic in twelve books, *The Idylls of the King*. (Interestingly, Wordsworth had himself been attracted by the idea of writing an Arthurian epic, but had rejected the project in favour of that much more unconventional work, *The Prelude*.) Prince Albert was particularly fond of *The Idylls*, and after his death Tennyson wrote a dedication which appears in later editions, a curiously touching act of homage, in which he describes Albert as

> Scarce other than my king's ideal knight . . .
> . . . Wearing the white flower of a blameless life.

The gallantry, the chivalry, the other-worldliness are haunting. It is surely no accident that one of the most famous of Tennyson's ballads tells the story of *The Lady of Shallot*, who could bear reality only when she saw it reflected in a mirror, and was doomed to death when she had the courage to seek the world at first hand, instead of through shadows. Reality was shocking; poetry passed it through a dimming and softening filter.

Matthew Arnold was another distinguished poet who found modern life disturbing; he took refuge in classical idylls and pastorals which are charged with his love of the English countryside. *The Scholar Gipsy*, like *The Lady of Shallot*, can only survive if he keeps well away from human society, with its mental strife, its 'sick hurry, its divided aims'. Like Tennyson, Arnold

53. Tennyson in medieval mood, photographed by his great friend
Julia Margaret Cameron.

experimented with the epic form, choosing an unusual subject
in his *Sohrab and Rustum*, taken from Persian legend and a
tenth-century Persian epic. He wanted to evoke a more heroic,
stirring age, as did William Morris in his treatment of the Ice-
landic sagas and his medieval ballads. Swinburne, Rossetti,
Meredith – they all harked back to a lost purity and heroism,
a lost energy. A famous poem by a largely forgotten writer
and classical scholar, Andrew Lang, sums up the Victorian
predicament; in his sonnet, *The Odyssey*, he complains of the
wan shadowy songs of modern speech, and expresses a yearning
for 'the surge and thunder of the Odyssey'. But the poem itself,

even while making this plea, is itself langorous and limp; Lang was, in his own words, lulled by the song of Circe. Reading through the Oxford Book of Victorian Verse, one might well imagine that its poets were, like Tennyson's lotos-eaters, locked under some strong enchantment, from which some would from time to time struggle to escape.

One or two brave spirits attempted different subjects. Elizabeth Barrett Browning, for example, wrote a long verse epic, immensely popular in its time, called *Aurora Leigh*, which is set defiantly in the mid-nineteenth century. It is crowded with social problems, plot, romance, melodrama and ideas, and its heroine Aurora is independent, a feminist, and a self-supporting writer, a far cry from Tennyson's patient maidens. At one point Aurora declares:

> I do distrust the poet who discerns
> No character or glory in his times,
> And trundles back his soul five hundred years,
> Past moat and drawbridge . . .
> Nay, if there's room for poets in this world,
> A little overgrown, (I think there is),
> Their sole work is to represent the age,
> Their age, not Charlemagne's.

This was a defiant claim, and *Aurora Leigh* does represent the age – but it is more novel than a poem, and reminds one at times of *Jane Eyre* in verse. Elizabeth's husband, Robert Browning, was another poet who avoided the languid, even when he was writing of historical characters. His work is rough, eccentric, obscure and aggressive. He rhymes not with the harmonious inevitability of a Tennyson or a Swinburne, but with startling eccentricity that demands close attention. Take the first verse of a short poem called *The Twins*:

> Grand rough old Martin Luther
> Bloomed fables – flowers on furze,
> The better the uncouther:
> Do roses stick like burrs?

It is very difficult to get any meaning out of these lines on a first reading. Browning's own poetry is rough and prickly like furze; what other writer would have dared to rhyme '*Luther*' with '*uncouther*'?

His subject matter is also far removed from a polite drawing-room standard; one of his best pieces is about a morgue in Paris, with detailed descriptions of corpses fished from the Seine. He prefers jaunty to soporific verse, and *How they brought the good news from Ghent to Aix* is a classic of lively metrical experiment. He loves to make learned and obscure allusions; there are many stories told against him, complaining of the incomprehensibility of his work. Even his friends complained; Jane Carlyle claimed to have read *Sordello* without discovering whether Sordello was a man, a city or a book. He was particularly fond of writing dramatic monologues, and brings to life a whole range of characters, speaking with their own distinctive voices, ranging from corrupt Renaissance bishops and dukes to Mr Sludge, a dishonest medium accused of cheating at a séance. Spiritualist séances were very popular at this period, and fooled many, including Browning's own wife, who seems genuinely to have believed that on one occasion 'spiritual hands took from the table a garland which lay there, and placed it upon my head'. Some commented that Browning's scepticism sprang from jealousy at this mysterious tribute, but one may reasonably assume that it was more deeply founded. Browning also wrote verse plays, with some success, and one wonders if in a different climate he might have become a dramatist rather than a poet. But serious Victorian drama hardly existed; the theatre had to wait for revival until the end of the century, when Ibsen and Chekhov were first seen in this country, and inspired dramatists like Shaw.

Browning was a religious optimist, who expressed his defiance of death and trust in God in many of his works, willingly accepting the imperfections of human life and understanding. But, significantly, the subject that most often roused his fellow Victorians to great poetry is that of religious conflict and despair. Tennyson's *In Memoriam* is a lengthy and moving attempt to accept the will of God after the death of his greatest friend. Gerard Manley Hopkins battled with God and doubt. He was a Roman Catholic convert, a Jesuit much influenced by the Oxford Movement of Newman. The loneliness of his life, and his struggles to reconcile his vocation as poet with his vocation as priest produced some of the finest religious poetry in the language. Sonnets such as *I wake and feel the fell of dark, not day*, describing his yearning for and wrestling with God, are not only extraordinarily original in technique; they have an intensity that had not been reached since the seventeenth century. Unfortunately, like Browning, he was ahead of his age, and unlike Browning, lacked the natural confidence and loyal friends that would have found him recognition as a great poet; his close friend, the poet Robert Bridges, whose own work was much more conventional, did not fully understand Hopkins's views on rhythm and language, and dissuaded him from seeking publication – a disaster, in worldly terms, for Hopkins himself and possibly for the development of English poetry, which badly needed daring and original writers to recharge a fading art. One can hardly doubt that it was the peculiar anguish of his position as a priest of a minority and once persecuted faith, cut off from family and support, that threw Hopkins with such violence against his feelings for God. He was passionately religious, but it was impossible for his poetry to show, except at rare moments, the quiet religious confidence that one finds in earlier poets such as George Herbert. It was difficult, in the nineteenth century, to be a simple believer; even more difficult to be a Roman Catholic. But conflict makes great poetry, at whatever cost to the poet.

Equally troubled by God, but less hopeful and therefore less passionate, were two other Victorian poets, Matthew Arnold and Thomas Hardy. Hardy, towards the end of the century, was to accuse his creator of deliberate malice or neglect towards mankind. He was deeply perplexed by the discoveries of modern science which seemed to dethrone God, yet could not quite accept that God did not exist – so perhaps God existed, and did not care? Many of his poems are worried, anxious inquiries into the nature of divine justice. The world, he says, is a dark and terrible place, cold and desolate, full of accident and tragedy. But Hardy cannot quite convince himself that the God of his childhood church-going days has vanished for ever, however vainly he seeks him, and a characteristic poem of his is *The Darkling Thrush*, set on an icy winter's day in a bleak landscape; the old bedraggled thrush starts to sing ecstatically in the gathering evening, and Hardy says that he sees so little cause for such joyous music that he might almost believe that

> There trembled through
> His happy good-night air
> Some blessed Hope, whereof he knew
> And I was unaware.

This is a characteristic cry of the nineteenth century, expressed here, as usually by Hardy, with a peculiar bleak honesty.

But perhaps the poem that best captures the religious doubts of the Victorians is by that peculiarly representative great Victorian, Matthew Arnold (see plate 54). Arnold, son of the headmaster of Rugby, a member of a hard-working, gifted, serious-minded family, also felt the loss of traditional faith. An intellectual, he could not dismiss the intellectual doubts of his day and throw himself, like Hopkins (and one of his own brothers) into Catholicism. Yet he suffered deeply from the loss of spiritual certainty. The harsh and ugly world of utilitarian materialism appalled him, and he wrote some fine essays on the British neglect of culture and pursuit of money; art and poetry were a refuge for him, and a standard, yet he could see that they were no adequate substitute for God. Perhaps his finest poem, *Dover Beach*, describes with honesty and dignity the failure of his attempts to find faith; it is a chilling and dignified farewell to God. Some of his other poems are over-decorated with up-to-date classical nymphs and shepherds, their sad messages disguised beneath a covering of purple orchises, pale mists, white evening stars and black-winged swallows, but *Dover Beach* speaks very simply, in plain language, of the 'sea of faith' which, the poet says, has now ebbed away. I know of no declaration more moving

54. Matthew Arnold, painted by G. F. Watts.

than that in the final stanza, where he says, having dismissed
the consolations of religion:

> Ah, love, let us be true
> To one another! for the world, which seems
> To lie before us like a land of dreams,
> So various, so beautiful, so new,
> Hath really neither joy, nor love, nor light,
> Nor certitude, nor peace, nor help for pain;
> And we are here as on a darkling plain
> Swept with confused alarums of struggle and flight,
> Where ignorant armies clash by night.

This is the voice of modern man, speaking calmly, clearly, and
stoically; one could almost imagine that in those last three lines

Arnold, gazing at Dover Beach, foresaw not the cheerful progress that Victorian optimists predicted, but the wars of the twentieth century.

Tennyson, Browning, Hopkins, Hardy, Arnold – these and a few others are the poets that we still read and remember. But there were also other, nameless poets, writing for the people, about entirely different subjects. Ballads and broadsheets with crudely rhymed but often lively verses were sold at street corners and in markets. The most popular subjects were murder and crime, always lurid, often fiction posing as fact. When Tennyson included a murder in his narrative poem *Locksley Hall* his readers protested and recoiled, but the readers of street ballads liked them to be as gory as possible. Religion and temperance were also common themes, though unlike Arnold and Hardy, the authors of these religious poems were always unquestioningly devout. Perhaps the most interesting, both historically and poetically, were those that dealt with politics or special events. Some of these were working-class protests about strikes or lockouts, but the majority were loyal and far from revolutionary in tone. The death of Wellington produced a piece with lines like:

> He's dead, our hero's gone to rest, and o'er his corpse we'll mourn,
> With sadness and with grief oppressed, for he will not return.

The Crystal Palace Exhibition inspired a patriotic poem of full praise for Old England's skills, a challenge to the Universe:

> The Sons of England and France
> And America likewise,
> With other nations do contend
> To bear away the prize.
> With pride depicted in their eyes,
> View the offspring of their hand,
> O, surely England's greatest wealth,
> Is an honest working man.

The name of one of these broadsheet writers has survived; the *Poetic Gems* of William McGonagall, whom Punch called 'the greatest Bad Verse writer of his age', have been reprinted many times, and have probably given as much unintentional pleasure as those of his more distinguished contemporaries. McGonagall, son of a Scottish weaver, left school at the age of seven and started work in a mill, but read widely in his spare time, developed a passion for Shakespeare and the theatre, and in 1877, in his own words: 'A flame, as Lord Byron has said, seemed to kindle up my entire frame, along with a strong desire to write poetry.' So he wrote, and recited and sold his little booklets of poetry to anyone who would listen or buy. He tackled a wide variety of subjects, historical, tragical, religious, and patriotic, and seems to have had a particular liking for shipwrecks. There is something endearingly naïve about his doggerel; it is hard to resist the charm of his lines on an *Attempted Assassination of the Queen*:

> Long may she be spared to roam
> Among the bonnie Highland floral,
> And spend many a happy day
> In the palace of Balmoral.
>
> Because she is very kind
> To the old women there,
> And allows them bread, tea and sugar,
> And each one gets a share.

Not great poetry, but a relief after the moaning doves and immemorial elms of the Poet Laureate.

THE NOVEL

Poetry was expected to deal with elevated themes. No wonder the Victorian poets found it difficult to write directly about their own turbulent, confusing, prosperous, money-making world. The novelist was in a much more fortunate position. He was allowed to deal with things as they really were. Never before had such a variety of human behaviour, such social contrasts, such dramatic rises and falls of fortune presented themselves to the writer, never before had he had so large and eager a reading public. The novel's prosperity coincides with the prosperity of the middle classes, for, largely, it was written by the middle classes for the middle classes. The novel was about real life – in it, the reader could read about ordinary people like himself, as well as a whole range of other characters, comic, criminal, grotesque, pathetic, destitute, wealthy. As a form (and a fairly new form, one must remember) it was immensely popular, and the most popular authors were those whom we still consider the best – readers waited eagerly for the next instalment of Dickens, Thackeray, Trollope, George Eliot, Mrs Gaskell, many of whose works were published in serial form in widely-distributed magazines. There was no gulf, as there is now, between the highbrow and the lowbrow – although, of course, plenty of romantic novels were being written by writers such as Mrs Henry Wood, whose sentimental *East Lynne* (1861) achieved great success, despite its implausibility. There was a vogue for historical novels, too, for readers, as well as art patrons, loved historical detail – but, as various critics have pointed out, Sir Walter Scott's heroes are really nineteenth-century gentlemen in fancy dress.

And the most successful Victorian novels dealt with contemporary subjects. Most of them are very long, packed with a wide variety of characters from different walks of life, full of sub-plots and diversions; like Victorian cities, they are crowded, bursting with energy, often untidy and unplanned, a strange mixture of beauty and squalor, of high life and low life. They are full of movement, unlike Frith's similarly crowded but frozen paintings; in Dickens's *Old Curiosity Shop*, we meet the same characters that Frith portrays in *Derby Day*, but while in *Derby Day* they are transfixed in a picturesque tableau, in Dickens the acrobats, the jugglers, the beggar children and the Punch and Judy troupe are full of humour, vitality and oddity. Sometimes the details are overcrowded, as they were on Pugin's churches; sometimes there are loose ends to the plot, melodramatic happenings, impossible solutions. The novel was not yet regarded as a serious art form, and it had no formal rules; it could be entertaining, descriptive, moral, educational, as it chose, and usually combined all these aspects. Towards the end of the century, Henry James condemned the Victorian novel as a baggy monster –

and some of them are monsters, but they are very lively ones. They may have dull patches, unanswered questions, unlikely coincidences, but so, as we all recognize, does life itself. The novels have none of Matthew Arnold's weary confusion in the face of 'this iron time of doubts, disputes, distractions, fears'; the Victorian novelist did not take refuge in a golden world of the past, but rushed into the real one, where poets feared to tread, along with the sanitary reformers and the feminists and the factory inspectors, tackling dirt, noise, crime, corruption, housing, scientific theories, female emancipation, electoral reform, the Trade Union Movement. (The only major topic they tended to avoid was sex; the most outspoken of them compromised with prevailing taste on this subject, and those who did not, like Hardy and Mrs Gaskell, quickly ran into censorship problems.)

We have already mentioned novelists, such as Disraeli and Mrs Gaskell, who wrote with an expressed desire to reform social evils. Others, such as Dickens and Trollope, sugared the pill of social criticism with humour and sentiment, and were better at exposing wrongs than at suggesting remedies for them. The Brontë sisters wrote from frustration, though Emily, in *Wuthering Heights*, produced a masterpiece that far transcends this description. The novels of Ann and Charlotte can be seen as personal protests about the plight of women in Britain. George Eliot's characters, Maggie Tulliver in *The Mill on the Floss* and Dorothea in *Middlemarch*, are also victims of society, and Mrs Gaskell, herself a happily married wife and mother wrote of the less fortunate in *Ruth* and *Mary Barton*, choosing working girls as her heroines. It is not surprising that so many nineteenth-century novels can be read as feminist protests – women were becoming articulate and angry, had few other outlets, and the novel was an ideal vehicle for their self-expression. Some men took their part, notably Thackeray, whose *Vanity Fair* portrayed in Becky Sharp a governess less virtuous than Jane Eyre, but equally exploited. *Ruth*, incidentally, is a good measure of the prudery of the time – it confronts the taboo subject of a girl who had an illegitimate baby. Mrs Gaskell writes in a thoroughly moral tone, and ends the book with Ruth's death, as, after a life of virtue and repentance, she nurses her one-time lover through a cholera epidemic – but this was not enough, and the book was denounced and burned by offended readers, as, years later, was Hardy's *Jude the Obscure*, which dared to question the institution of marriage.

George Eliot (1819–1880) has been recognized by many as the greatest of Victorian novelists (see plate 55). Her mature works provide a magnificently full picture of English life. Her real name was Mary Ann Evans; she published under a male pen-name (as did the Brontës) partly to spare the feelings of her family, partly because she felt women writers were not taken as seriously

55. A daguerrotype of George Eliot.

as men. She was an independent, widely-read, liberal-minded woman, whose work shows many of the qualities we think of as typical of Victorian intellectuals – an almost scientific curiosity about human nature and psychology, a deep moral earnestness coupled with a scepticism about traditional Christian beliefs, a desire for improvement and progress together with a respect for the past, particularly the past of the English countryside. She was brought up in the country, in the Midlands, and loved to describe age-old pursuits and amusements; she writes of the village inn, the dairy, of fishing expeditions, of gipsies, tinkers, millers and carpenters, drawing on childhood memories. Yet she sensed that the old ways were dying, and although she describes childhood as a time of happiness, it was a happiness that could not last. Country people may be picturesque, but they are also stubborn, harsh and narrow-minded. She moved away from her roots to the freer, more stimulating intellectual life of London. But regret for the past lingers, as it does in the novels of Hardy, another countryman who detested the narrow prejudices of provincial life, yet longed for the lost harmony of old England – the 'Merrie England' which maybe never existed, except on odd summer afternoons during a good harvest.

Both Hardy and George Eliot had mixed and complex feelings about change, and the impact of machinery on traditional ways of life; for both the coming of the railway stands as an important symbol. In *Middlemarch* there is a description of farm labourers in their smocks confronting four railway surveyors, and threatening them with their hayforks – a fine image of the resentment that the old world felt for the new. But protest as it might, the peasant world, unchanged for centuries, was about to disappear for ever, and George Eliot knew it; as Caleb Garth, the land agent, says to the labourers, 'You can't hinder the railroad: it will be made whether you like it or not. And if you go fighting against it, you'll get yourselves into trouble.' In *Tess of the D'Urbevilles* there is a scene where dairymaid Tess, a classic victim of the mechanization of farm labour, drives with her lover Angel Clare to the railway station to deliver the milk in the spring-wagon; Hardy points out the contrast between the hissing train, with its gleaming cranks and wheels, and 'this unsophisticated girl, with the round bare arms, the rainy face and hair . . . the print gown of no date or fashion, and the cotton bonnet drooping on her brow'. Modern life, he says, in a striking image, 'stretched out its steam feeler three or four times a day, touched the native existences, and quickly withdrew its feeler again . . .' Tess, on the way home, wonders at the thought of Londoners she had never seen drinking the milk from her own dairy. In *Phyllis's Lover*, Mrs Gaskell uses the same symbol when she describes the heartbreak of a farmer's daughter who falls in love with a visiting railway engineer.

Such contrasts make us realize how shocking and sudden the change from rural to industrial England seemed to the Victorians; in one generation, the whole face of the countryside altered. The railways, carrying newspapers, new ideas, and mass-produced goods from London to the remotest spots, as well as milk from Dorset to London, dramatically accelerated the rate of change. The writers of the time felt a two-fold impulse – to document the process of change itself, and to record, before it vanished, a dying England.

On the whole, however, George Eliot was a progressive, like most of the novelists. She welcomed democracy and the reform bills; one of her heroes, Felix Holt, is a working-class radical. Her novels demonstrate women's need for education and useful employment. She saw the importance of increasing scientific knowledge, and another hero, Dr Lydgate, battles bravely against the kind of ignorant superstitious prejudice that hindered Chadwick, Simon and Snow. She was firmly on the side of enlightenment. Although of a naturally religious temperament, she could see that blind faith in Christianity and the Bible were no longer sufficient; in 1846 she translated from the German Strauss's *Life of Jesus*, a book which shocked the orthodox world by questioning the historical truth of the Gospels. Like many intellectual Victorians, she managed to replace Christianity by a personal religion of moral duty and social conscience. But she reflected, in her own life, the great doubts of the day, and brings us to what must be our last section.

꧁꧁꧁꧁꧁

DARWIN AND DOUBT

꧁꧁꧁꧁꧁

FOR me, the greatest single discovery of the nineteenth century
was the discovery of the theory of evolution. In an age so packed
with invention, it is perhaps unfair to single out one achievement,
but the theories of Charles Darwin had such an overwhelming
effect on the lives and imaginations of the whole world, and are
still so deeply disturbing to us, that they present a special case.
Most scientific discoveries alter our material environment,
sometimes very profoundly, but Darwin's altered our whole
conception of the universe. He shattered our safe, familiar picture
of a universe with man as its centre and God as its creator, and
replaced it with something frightening and uncomfortable – a
world in which man appeared as a tiny pigmy, descended from
unwanted apelike ancestors, struggling for survival in a hostile
rather than a friendly environment, on his way towards some
unknown goal (possibly extinction), driven there not by reason
and moral virtue, but by deep, selfish animal instincts.

God did not fit comfortably into this new plan. Before Darwin
most people, scientists included, had believed in the literal truth
of the Bible, which told them in the Book of Genesis that God
had created the world in six days, only a few thousand years ago;
some thought that the year could be fixed exactly at 4004 BC. They
also believed he had made each species of creature individually,
in a fixed and unchangeable mould. Men, giraffes, tortoises,
spiders, whales – God had Himself designed a pattern for each
one. Darwin declared, though not in so many words, that the
Bible was wrong. The world was immeasurably older than the

Bible supposed, and the forms of life in it, far from having been copied from an original model like animals in a Noah's Ark, had developed slowly over the millennia, adapting themselves to changing natural conditions. The impact of this revelation was stunning. Some were simply unable to accept it. The conflict between religious faith and scientific enlightenment is described most readably and vividly in Edmund Gosse's *Father and Son*, mentioned earlier; Gosse's father was a respected zoologist, and all his professional sense lead him, in the 1850s, to welcome the new theories – 'every instinct in his intelligence', says his son, 'went out at first to greet the new light'. But he was also a dogmatic Christian, and his loyalty to Genesis destroyed his scientific judgement; to justify his rejection of evolution, he produced a ridiculous counter-theory, which accounted for the problem of fossils by claiming that God, at the creation, had planted them ready-made in the rocks. It was mocked by atheists and Christians alike, and Gosse senior was left in a spiritual and scientific wilderness, where he suffered great agony of mind. His was an extreme case, but his anxieties were shared by many.

There are signs that Darwin appreciated the explosive nature of the bombshell he had prepared in his *On the Origin of Species,* which was published in 1859. He had been working on his theories for many years, since his voyage of discovery in the *Beagle* in 1834, but was slow to publish his findings, realizing they would be unacceptable, and wanting to check and test them as thoroughly as possible. He knew he would shock; in a letter to his friend Joseph Hooker, director of Kew Gardens, he says that confessing to doubts of the immutability of species was like 'confessing a murder'. Naturalists clung the more obstinately to their old beliefs, the more the evidence against them piled up, and it was heresy to suggest that species could change and develop, and had been doing so since life began No wonder Darwin was reluctant to attack such cherished opinions. He was finally pushed into declaring his views by a letter from a young scientist, Alfred Russell Wallace, who had worked out a theory of natural selection very similar to his own; Darwin consulted his friends, who urged him to publish, and in 1858 he and Wallace presented their findings together to the Royal Society, like true gentlemen. In his own life, Darwin certainly did not demonstrate the spirit of competition and struggle for survival which his works explain; he was modest and patient, and wrote of Wallace's discovery: 'I would far rather burn my whole book than that he or any other man should think that I behaved in a paltry spirit.' Did he recognize that he had himself cast the gravest doubt on the possibility of real human generosity and altruism? And if he did, did he attempt to behave all the more nobly in his private life as some kind of counter-demonstration? Many modern philosophers have found themselves forced to take the position that, although God does not exist, it is necessary to behave as though He did – and perhaps unconsciously Darwin may have felt this too. He had discovered natural laws that seemed to excuse savage and ruthless competition, as the only means to avoid extinction, and was therefore all the more determined to show that he could act unselfishly himself.

He did not, of course, make his discoveries single-handed. Others had been working on the same lines. Lyell's *Principles of Geology*, suggesting that the world was unthinkably ancient, was published in 1830. The French zoologist Lamarck, in 1801, and Patrick Matthew in 1832 had written of the theory of natural selection; the views of the latter were very similar to Darwin's, as Darwin admits, but nobody took much notice of them. Herbert Spencer, philosopher and close friend of George Eliot, had his own views on the evolution of the mind, and was responsible for coining the phrase 'the survival of the fittest'. The theories on population and subsistence developed by Malthus also impressed Darwin. So the theory of evolution was very much in the air in the mid-nineteenth century, and came as an answer to many long-debated problems. Nevertheless, the chief credit goes to Darwin himself; his enthusiastic supporter T. H. Huxley writes that *On the Origin of Species* came upon him like a flash of light in the darkness, and that his first thought after grasping its message was 'How extremely stupid not to have thought of that!'

And there is something wonderfully obvious about the concept. Unlike some great intellectual discoveries, it can be grasped, at least in broad outline, by almost anyone. We have all heard of Einstein's theory of relativity, but few of us could give an account of it, whereas we all know that the world is billions of years old, that it was once inhabited by dinosaurs, pterodactyls and other extinct monsters, and that men are descended from monkeys. These facts are familiar to any reader of comics, to any television viewer, to any visitor to a natural history museum. Dinosaurs caught the popular imagination at once, and have appeared in many forms, from Conan Doyle's *The Lost World* to *The Flintstones*. It is hard to remember that before 1859 these facts would have been considered ridiculous and blasphemous fancies. The delight that cartoonists took in ridiculing Darwin's discoveries (see plate 56) only helped to spread them. His audience was not a group of learned scientists, but the whole nation. And by and large, we all accept his theories as true – though there are still religious sects who ban his works, and occasional scientists who remind us that evolution is a hypothesis, not a tested fact. Most Christians now read the Bible and the Book of Genesis as poetic metaphor rather than literal truth; humanists believe man's moral sense is as natural and deeply rooted as his desire for survival. Few people are now at all shocked by the idea that we are related to chimpanzees; on the contrary, television programmes that point out the similarities between human and animal behaviour are now highly popular, as are programmes about archeology that describe man's most ancient ancestors. We have accepted and assimilated a new world view, though we are still at work adjusting its details.

Nor did the new theory bring nothing but doubt and despair. Some, like Huxley, found it beautiful, liberating, a new life-blood. The sense of intellectual adventure was immensely exciting; Lyell, on hearing Darwin's account of coral reef formation, 'was so overcome with delight that he danced about and threw himself into the wildest contortions, as was his manner when excessively pleased'. In our own day, some of us remember the joy which greeted that strange fish, the Coelecanth,

56. A contemporary cartoon poking fun at
Darwin's theory of evolution.

which was hailed as the missing link in the evolutionary chain.
Darwin opened our eyes to the beauty and diversity of nature,
and inspired the spirit of enthusiasm expressed in the flower
paintings of Marianne North (1830–1890), an intrepid spinster
from the South of England who travelled to the remotest parts
of the world, recording hundreds of rare species (see colour
plate 9); it was at Darwin's own suggestion that she included
Australia and New Zealand in her itinerary. Her work is a tribute
to the richness of life and its myriad strange manifestations, com-
bining scientific curiosity and fidelity with a sense of admiration.

For her at least, Darwin's discoveries proved stimulating rather than depressing. The Victorians were naturally interested in natural history, and the Museum in South Kensington, with its prehistoric monsters and Blue Whale, is an enduring and ever-popular monument to their eager desire for information, and their sense of wonder. Darwin himself had started off humbly as a beetle collector, and the passion for collecting eggs, fossils, insects and shells was given a new thrill and importance. Darwin loved his work, and corresponded enthusiastically with amateur pigeon fanciers, with gardeners and breeders of dogs; he was at home in his newly discovered animal kingdom. Contemporary drawings show him strolling in his garden, surrounded by small creatures, with squirrels running up his coat. This was no godless pessimist, surely; had he not rather revealed God's creative ingenuity? His own words, from the last paragraph of *On the Origin of Species*, show his spirit of reverence and love. He writes:

> It is interesting to contemplate a tangled bank, clothed with many plants of many kinds, with birds singing on the bushes, with various insects flitting about, and with worms crawling through the damp earth, and to reflect that these elaborately constructed forms, so different from each other, and dependent upon each other in so complex a manner, have all been produced by laws acting around us ... There is grandeur in this view of life, with its several powers, having been originally breathed by the Creator into a few forms or into one; and that, whilst this planet has gone cycling on according to the fixed law of gravity, from so simple a beginning endless forms most beautiful and most wonderful have been, and are being evolved.

Darwin saw his own studies as interesting, noble, improving: 'I see no good reason,' he says, 'why the views given in this volume should shock the religious feeling of anyone.'

And yet, and yet ... we all alternate between optimism and pessimism, and so does history. For me at least, the most resounding note of the Victorian age is, after all, one of dignified resignation. Man had gained the whole world, but lost his own soul. Never again would he be able to feel the ancient certainties. Never again would he be able to place himself but a little lower than the angels. George Eliot could no longer hope for heaven or immortality; she had to content herself with a vision of living on through her works, in the lives of others. Her poem, *The Choir Invisible*, seems to renounce personal joy and individual salvation for a more communal, selfless 'evolutionary' concept of progress and goodness; she says that the music of the invisible choir of the dead is 'the gladness of the world', but the tone of her poem is earnest and doubtful, rather than glad, as though seeking some consolation for loss.

And Matthew Arnold looked at Dover Beach, a few years after Darwin's bombshell, and wrote:

> The sea of faith
> Was once, too, at the full, and round earth's shore
> Lay like the folds of a bright girdle furl'd.
> But now I only hear
> Its melancholy, long, withdrawing roar,
> Retreating to the breath
> Of the night-wind down the vast edges drear
> And naked shingles of the world.

Which was the Victorian age; a grassy bank teeming with life, warmed by the sun of prosperity, an endlessly fascinating spectacle – or a naked shingle? That melancholy, long withdrawing roar echoes behind much of what we read of Victorian life, and echoes still today.

꧑꧑꧑꧑꧑

BIBLIOGRAPHY

꧑꧑꧑꧑꧑

I. SOURCE MATERIAL

Bell, Quentin. *Victorian Artists*. Academy Editions, London, 1975

Briggs, Asa. *Victorian Cities*. Penguin, Harmondsworth, 1968
—*Victorian People: A Reassessment of Persons and Themes 1851–67*. University of Chicago Press, Illinios, 1975

Clark, Kenneth. *The Gothic Revival*. Harper & Row, New York, 1974

Conrad, Peter. *The Victorian Treasure House*. Collins, London, 1973

Cooper, Nicholas. *The Opulent Eye*. Watson-Guptill Publications, New York, 1977

Gerin, Winifred. *Anne Brontë: A Biography*. Rowman & Littlefield, New Jersey, 1975
—*Charlotte Brontë: The Evolution of Genius*. Oxford University Press (Oxford Paperbacks), New York, 1967
—*Elizabeth Gaskell: A Biography*. Oxford University Press, New York, 1976
—*Emily Brontë: A Biography*. Oxford University Press, New York, 1972

Girouard, Mark. *The Victorian Country House*. Oxford University Press, New York, 1971

Gloag, John. *Victorian Comfort: A Social History of Designs, 1830–1900*. David and Charles, Vermont, 1976

Hayter, Alethea. *A Sultry Month: Scenes of London Literary Life in 1846*. Faber & Faber, London, 1965

Hilton, Timothy. *The Pre-Raphaelites*. Abrams, New York, 1971

Jeal, Tim. *David Livingstone*. Dell, New York, 1974

Longford, Elizabeth. *Victoria R.I.* Harper & Row, New York, 1973

Morley, John (Ed.). *Death, Heaven and the Victorians*. University of Pittsburgh Press, 1972

Neuburg, Victor E. *Popular Literature: A History and Guide*. Penguin (Pelican) Harmondsworth, 1977

Pevsner, Nikolaus. *Pioneers of Modern Design*. Penguin Books, New York, 1961

Pike, Edgar Royston (Ed.). *Golden Times: Human Documents of the Victorian Age*. Schocken, New York, 1972

Pinchbeck, Ivy and Hewitt, Margaret. *Children in English Society: Vol. 2: From the Eighteenth Century to the Children Act of 1948*. University of Toronto Press, Toronto, 1972

Strachey, Lytton. *Eminent Victorians*. Putnam, New York, 1963
—*Queen Victoria*. Harcourt Brace, New York, 1949.

Schaefer, Herwin. *Roots of Modern Design: Functional Tradition in the Nineteenth Century*. Studio Vista, London, 1970

Smith, Cecil Woodham. *Queen Victoria: Her Life and Times*. Hamish Hamilton, London, 1972 and Collins (Fontana), London, 1969 (paperback)

Vicinus, Martha J. (Ed.). *Suffer and Be Still: Women in the Victorian Age*. Indiana University Press, Indiana, 1972

Young, G. M. *Victorian England: Portrait of an Age*. Oxford University Press, New York, 1964

2. LITERATURE OF THE TIME

Alcott, Louisa M. *Little Women*. Penguin Books, New York, 1954

Arnold, Matthew. *Culture and Anarchy*. Cambridge University Press, Cambridge, 1932
—*Poetry and Prose*. Edited by Sir Edmund K. Chambers. Oxford University Press, New York, 1939

Brontë, Charlotte. *Jane Eyre*. New American Library, New York, 1971

Browning, Robert. *Selected Verse*. Edited by W. F. Williams. Penguin Books, New York, 1976

Carlyle, Jane. *Letters and Memorials of Jane Welsh Caryle, 2 vols*. AMS Press, 1903

Carroll, Lewis. *Alice in Wonderland* and *Through the Looking Glass*, Illustrated by Sir John Tenniel. Macmillan, New York, 1927 and Penguin Books, New York, 1946

Darwin, Charles. *The Origin of Species*. Macmillan, New York, 1962

Dickens, Charles. *Great Expectations*. Penguin Books, New York, 1969
—*Oliver Twist*. Penguin Books, New York, 1966
—*The Old Curiosity Shop*. Penguin Books, New York, 1972

Eliot, George. *Adam Bede*. Dutton, New York
—*Middlemarch*. Penguin Books, New York, 1965
—*The Mill on the Floss*. Dutton, New York, 1956

Emerson, R. W. *English Traits*. Harvard University Press, Cambridge, Mass., 1966

Engels, Friedrich. *The Condition of the Working Class in England*. Path Press, New York

Gaskell, Mrs. E. C. *Cranford*. Penguin, Harmondsworth, 1976
—*Mary Barton*. Dutton, New York, 1961
—*North and South*. Scholarly Press, Michigan, 1971

Gosse, Edmund. *Father and Son*. Norton, New York, 1963

Hardy, Thomas. *Tess of the D'Urbevilles*. Dell, New York

Hopkins, G. M. *Poems and Prose*. Peter Smith, Mass., 1973

Hughes, Thomas. *Tom Brown's Schooldays*. Penguin Books, New York, 1972

Jefferies, Richard. *Bevis : The Story of a Boy*. Puffin, Harmondsworth, 1974

Kingsley, Charles. *The Water Babies*. Illustrated by Heath Robinson. Dutton, New York, 1977

MacBeth, George (Ed.). *The Penguin Book of Victorian Verse*. Penguin, Harmondsworth, 1969

Mayhew, Henry. *London Labour and the London Poor*. 4 vols. Peter Smith, Mass.

Newman, Cardinal John Henry. *Apologia Pro Vita Sua*. Doubleday, New York, 1977

Pugin, A. W. N. *Contrasts*. Leicester University Press, Leicester, 1969

Ruskin, John. *Ruskin Today*. Edited by Kenneth Clark. Penguin, Harmondsworth, 1967

Stowe, Harriet Beecher. *Uncle Tom's Cabin*. Dutton, New York, 1961

Tennyson, Alfred. *Choice of Verse*. Edited by Lord David Cecil. Faber, London, 1971 (paperback)

Thackeray, W. M. *Vanity Fair*. Penguin Books, New York, 1969

Trollope, Anthony. *The Way We Live Now*. Oxford University Press, New York, 1974

Victoria, Queen. *Letters*. John Murray, London, 1907–32

3. FICTION FOR THE SAME AGE GROUP

Avery, Gillian. *A Likely Lad*. Collins (Armada Lions), London, 1973

Bull, Angela. *Child of Ebenezer*. Collins, London, 1974

Chambers, Peggy. *The Governess*. Penguin (Peacock), Harmondsworth, 1964

Cookson, Catherine. *Our John Willie*. New American Library, New York, 1975

Darke, Marjorie. *Ride the Iron Horse*. Collins (Armada Lions), London, 1975

Grice, Frederick. *The Bonnie Pit Laddie*. Oxford University Press, London, 1966

Jefferies, Richard. *Bevis : The Story of a Boy*. Puffin, Harmondsworth, 1974

Johnson, Annabel and Edgar. *Torrie*. Harper & Row, New York, 1960

McPherson, Margaret. *Battle of the Braes*. Collins, London, 1972

Price, Susan. *Tuppence a Tub*. Faber, London, 1975

Schlee, Ann. *Ask Me No Questions*. Macmillan, London, 1976

Symons, Geraldine. *The Workhouse Child*. Macmillan, New York, 1971

Willard, Barbara. *The Warden's Niece*. Collins, London, 1957

INDEX